This book is dedicated to my wife Padmini and daughter Supriya, as a partial repayment of all that I have received from them.

ACKNOWLEDGMENTS

Swami Sadashiva Brahmendra, Chennai, India for his blessings

Avinash Gokhale, Pune, India for having goaded into writing on Bridge

Jeff Rubens, Editor of *The Bridge World*. He did not know me from Adam, but gave me all the introductions I needed

Dr Ron Garber, Temicula, CA, USA. He was instrumental in the publication of my first book on Bridge

Roger Huggins, Publisher, B.T. Batsford, UK

Elena Jeronimidis, Editor of *Bridge Plus*, UK

Tony Gordon, UK

Professor Mayank Dholakiya, Baroda, India

Sunil Machhar, Bombay, India

K. Krishnakumar, Chennai, India

Archie Sequeira, Bombay, India

P. Sridhar, Chennai, India

S. Sundar Ram, Chennai, India

B. Prabhakar, Virudhunagar, India

R. Krishnan, Chennai, India

Raju Tolani, Bombay, India

Ajay Khare, Bombay, India

Anil Padhye, Bombay, India

Sunit Choksi, Ahmedabad, India

And, last but not least, my dear friend Arun Kochar, who has been a great cheer-leader

INTRODUCTION

Nearly two decades ago, Jagdeesh Sardesai, a good friend of mine, told me that it is not always that one gets to do the work one likes – but, he also told me, a time will definitely come in everyone's life when one does get an opportunity to do the work one likes. Prophetic words.

Working on this book is something that I have enjoyed enormously. I do hope it gives the reader as much pleasure as I had writing it.

In my first book, *Logic, Intuition and Instinct at the Bridge Table*, I postulated that there is more to Bridge than mere logical thinking and that intuition does play an important part now and then. I raised questions but I had no answers to offer. I had given examples of play for which there was no logical explanation, but that was as far as I could go. What I tried to suggest in that book was that "trying to choose between reason and intuition, or between head and heart, is like trying to walk on one leg or to see with one eye."

In a very broad sense, this book is a sequel to that thought process. Late one evening last year, I stumbled upon the word 'serendipity' – not that I had not heard the word before – and suddenly the word had a new meaning for me. What struck me was that there are some things that impinge on us day in and day out and, in a way, they have a definitive influence on all the actions that we take every day. As James Redfield so magnificently put it in his classic book *The Celestine Prophecy* (Warner Books, 1997) there are "dormant receptors within us . . . we have to be constantly aware of the coincidences that happen in our lives."

These coincidences, these 'somethings' that strike us, are all happenings over which we have no control. They happen nevertheless, ostensibly to enable us to "discover the unexpected," as Professor Mayank Dholakiya says in his treatise which appears in this book. As the Professor puts it so beautifully, "as we stumble upon events, each event can become the basis of subsequent insight."

These events, these 'somethings' which strike us and these coincidences all lead us to moments of truth which can be seen as critical decision points when we make unexpected discoveries, particularly when we were not looking for them.

I believe that these 'moments of truth' have eminent applicability at the Bridge table and it is that belief which prompted me to write this book. Sunil Machhar dropping the doubleton queen against all odds ("Disarm That Intuition"), Prabhakar playing the jack holding A-Q-J-x-x opposite a singleton ("Cards Can Scream"), Archie Sequeira 'drawing' a singleton ace of trumps by playing a small trump when he is missing A-Q-10-9-x ("A Visual(isation) treat"), Raju Tolani entering the bidding with all of seven high-card points in the sixth round of a bidding sequence when the opponents were bidding themselves to glory ("Inferential Bidding"), may all be instances where the players have been influenced by intuition. It behoves all of us, however, to accept that such spectacularly successful plays and bids were not in the reckoning in the minds of these players even seconds before they made the play, or bid, at the table. It is my considered opinion that what must have happened in the thought processes of these players were 'sudden strikes,' strikes they must have discovered unexpectedly at those particular points in time. These particular points in time are indeed moments of truth.

It will do all of us a lot of good to remember that it is not enough to be merely aware of what is happening to us or around us. We need to be wide awake to such happenings because, more often than not, they are pointers leading us to the right path.

R. Jayaram
Baroda, India
June 2003

CONTENTS

CONTENTS continued

DISARM THAT INTUITION!

During the Indian Masters tournament at Bombay in October 2002, Sunil Machhar and I were having a *tête-à-tête* on intuition at the Bridge table. As often happens in such passionate discussions, suddenly and without warning, something very interesting cropped up. Sunil is a keen Bridge player and an Indian Master. He regularly sponsors his own team in major Indian tournaments and has tucked away quite a few trophies, including the Indian Masters. He is a man of very few words, a good listener and when he does speak, he speaks incisively. He is a past master in the art of dropping singleton kings and doubleton queens at the table, against the odds. Like me, he believes with conviction that intuition is an integral and inescapable part of the game. In fact, he goes one step further, and says that intuition is a reality in almost everything that we do in our lives. When I ventured to quote Professor Mayank Dholakiya from my first book* that "it is illogical to pretend that intuition is an illusion," he simply said: "Precisely."

In the league stages of a major Indian tournament a couple of years back, Sunil was in 7◊ and against the odds he dropped the doubleton queen in the other minor to walk away with the winner's prize. Later in the evening, Master after Indian Master ridiculed Sunil's line of play as being totally out of step with distribution probabilities. "Sunil was just lucky," was the uniform verdict. The deal and the story as told to me by Sunil and later by another Indian Master, S.K. Iyengar, follows.

Logic, Intuition, and Instinct at the Bridge Table, Vivisphere Publishing, Poughkeepsie, NY, 2001

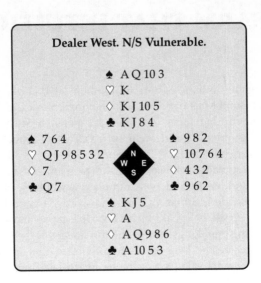

Dealer West. N/S Vulnerable.

```
              ♠ A Q 10 3
              ♡ K
              ◇ K J 10 5
              ♣ K J 8 4
♠ 7 6 4                      ♠ 9 8 2
♡ Q J 9 8 5 3 2     N        ♡ 10 7 6 4
◇ 7             W       E     ◇ 4 3 2
♣ Q 7               S        ♣ 9 6 2
              ♠ K J 5
              ♡ A
              ◇ A Q 9 8 6
              ♣ A 10 5 3
```

Contract: 7◇ by South. Lead: ♡Q.

Taking advantage of the favourable vulnerability, West had opened a pre-emptive 3♡, but that did not prevent Sunil and partner from reaching the grand slam in diamonds. The duplication in hearts was heart-rending but the contract obviously hinged on locating the queen of clubs.

Winning the heart lead, Sunil drew three rounds of trumps and cashed four spade winners discarding a club from hand. He then cashed his last two diamonds, discarding a club from dummy. West had followed to three spades and one diamond, and discarded five hearts on the rest of the winners, the last one being the nine of hearts. East had followed to three spades and three diamonds and discarded three hearts, the last one being the ten of hearts. The count was complete. With the hand holding A-10-5 of clubs to play, dummy holding K-J-8, it was clear to Sunil that East held three clubs, and West two clubs and the jack of hearts.

Sunil now played the five of clubs to the king on the table; the seven appeared from the left and the deuce from the right. The odds had now become two-to-one for East to hold the queen. Sunil saw the six of clubs from the right as he plays the second club from the table, but intuitively went up with the ace to drop the queen on his left!

"The anti-percentage play of the year," commented a kibitzer.

"Why, was there any specific reason?" I asked Sunil during our *tête-à-tête*. "None that I can justify even today," replied Sunil.

Post-Mortem

In a private gathering later in the evening after the event, S. K Iyengar, an Indian Master, was quietly listening to the "injured-pride-tirade" against Sunil that was going on. If Sunil is a man of few words, Iyengar is a man of few half words. And Iyengar was smiling, even as he cleared his throat to speak. When Iyengar speaks, the rest of the Indian Bridge fraternity listens.

"Just a point of view. At a very critical Trick Ten, East knew everything that he needed to know. In fact, he knew one thing that South did not.

"He knew he had to persuade the declarer to take the losing finesse through him. How, was the question. On the last diamond, if East were to discard the two of clubs instead of that tell-tale ten of hearts, what would declarer conclude? Would it not be logical and reasonable for South to conclude that all *four* cards in the East hand were clubs?

"West had opened a super light 3♡ and using the very basic n-minus-three principle, would it not make a little more sense for him to have an eight-card heart suit? In this case, there was the possibility, indeed the danger of intuition working (the declarer was the proverbial 'queen-dropper') and the only hope for East was to disarm that intuition. Only overwhelming logic can halt intuition."

Sunil ambled across to where Iyengar was sitting, and patted him on the back. Often, actions are more eloquent than words.

> "I changed my mind," an intuitionist might say. A logician? Never, ever.

LESSER RISK,
NOT THE WHOLE STORY

Almost disarmingly friendly and very likeable, K. Krishnakumar (KK to the Indian Bridge fraternity) is a technocrat by profession and an Indian Master in Bridge. Having been a member of the winning team in the 42nd Indian Nationals held in January 2001, he was well on his way to a back-to-back title in the 43rd Indian Nationals held at Calcutta in December, 2001 with just two matches to go. Along came Board 26 in the 64-boards semi-finals and KK was in 4♠:

Dealer East. Both Vulnerable.

♠	8 6 5 3
♡	K 9 7
◇	J 8 2
♣	K Q 5

```
      N
  W       E
      S
```

♠	K Q J 9 4
♡	A
◇	A Q
♣	J 9 7 3 2

West	North	East	South
		Pass	1♣
Pass	1NT	Pass	2♠
Pass	3♠	Pass	4♠
All Pass			

Contract: 4♠ by South. Lead: ♣10.

KK and his partner were playing the Precision Club bidding system without the asking bids and the auction was simple and straight-forward. K K called for the king from the table on the lead of the ten of clubs and East, Debasish Roy (a ranked World Master) took his ace (rather too quickly, I thought) and shot back the four of diamonds.

KK went into a trance. I could vaguely see that he was afraid of a club ruff. If he finesses the diamond now and it loses, back comes another club, and if the trump ace is with East, the contract might go down via a third-round club ruff. How about winning with the diamond ace, cash the ace of hearts, and then play a second club to dummy to take a diamond discard on the king of hearts? That would not do if the ten of clubs were a singleton. Declarer knew that West was short in clubs, but East had no means of knowing that, certainly not at that juncture in the play. If indeed that diamond lead was a singleton, West would have a great story to tell his grandchildren: "No, my partner did not give me a ruff. He developed a trick for me in another suit and *then* declarer gave me a ruff!"

KK won the diamond switch with the ace and cashed the ace of hearts. Would you, if you were declarer, play a second club to the table to take a diamond discard on the king of hearts? The chances of West following to the second round of clubs would seem to be in the region of 3-to-1 as there are three possible doubleton holdings (10-8, 10-6, 10-4) compared to the one possible singleton holding (10). But do you need that? What are your losers? On the face of it, a club, a diamond and the ace of trumps. Narrowing down to the conclusions that (a) if West has the trump ace, he cannot get a ruff, and (b) if West has more than one club he still cannot get a ruff, KK played the king of spades at Trick Four and East . . . discarded a heart!

The full deal:

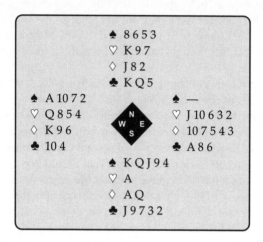

```
                    ♠ 8 6 5 3
                    ♡ K 9 7
                    ◇ J 8 2
                    ♣ K Q 5
   ♠ A 10 7 2                      ♠ —
   ♡ Q 8 5 4         N            ♡ J 10 6 3 2
   ◇ K 9 6      W         E       ◇ 10 7 5 4 3
   ♣ 10 4           S             ♣ A 8 6
                    ♠ K Q J 9 4
                    ♡ A
                    ◇ A Q
                    ♣ J 9 7 3 2
```

KK lost 13 IMPs on the deal which was the margin of his team's ultimate defeat in that semi-final. In the same contract at the other table, the opening lead was a heart.

Let us get into a fictitious conversation, with you as the declarer.

"Can you make the contract if the clubs are 1-4?"

"Yes, I can, provided the trump ace is with West and provided further he does not hold all four trumps."

"Can you make the contract if West holds all four trumps?"

"Yes, I can, provided clubs break 2-3 *and* I make the right choice of play at Trick Four."

"Are you aware that the combined probability percentages of two suit-patterns can be worked out mathematically?"

"Yes, but that is far too complicated to work out at the table."

"Did you have evidence, any evidence at all, as to how the suits are likely to break at the point at which you had to decide on a plan? "

"No, none at all."

"But you knew the probability percentages?"

"Yes"

"The probability percentages of two suits in isolation, not together?"

"Yes, clubs breaking 2-3 was originally a 68% probability and spades *not* breaking 4-0, which was what I needed, a 90% probability. Actually, as I can cope with all four spades on the right by finessing against the ten, I was OK unless West held all four trumps and this line had a 95% probability. Logically, the latter is better"

"Is it as simple as that?"

"No. What had happened in the club suit had changed the probabilities, and even if West does not have all four trumps, there was *still* the possibility that East could give West a club ruff."

"So what plan would you have chosen?"

"The same as KK's."

"And lost?"

"As luck would have it, yes."

Much later, I had a lengthy discussion with KK himself on the play of the deal. As we were about to take leave of each other, I asked KK: "One last question. Very simply put, why did you not try a second club?"

He replied: "I may contradict myself, but this is what I felt at the time. One, I had to avoid a club ruff. Two, when all was said and done, the way I played it, I still retained the possibility of West having a second club. Three – and this was the most important consideration – at the table, I thought that playing on spades was only a 5% risk. I agree that it is more complicated than that and there is an inference, as I realised much later, that the perceived 5% risk is not the whole story. But in an eight-minute board, how deep an analysis can you really make? It is deals like this that make the game so fascinating. You win some, you also lose some. It has happened before and it will happen again."

KK had succeeded in disarming me for the umpteenth time.

In all these back-and-forth discussions, we may lose sight of a very important defensive point of view, which Debasish Roy (East) pointed out to me. "I was looking at a void in trumps in my hand and dummy's highest was the eight spot. As little as queen-ten to four cards with partner will give us two trump tricks, so it was important for us to develop a red suit winner before trumps were tackled. Hence the hurry in taking the ace of clubs." Even more interestingly, even if the ten of clubs were a singleton, the diamond switch was needed to defeat the contract. Very interestingly, as the cards lie, the *only* defence that can beat this contract is to duck the first club, win the second round of the suit and immediately play back a diamond!

> Probability percentages are effective tools in most cases. Repeat, most cases. Hence the word, 'probability.'

GIVE PARTNER A CHANCE

THE DATE AND PLACE:
16th December, 2001. Netaji Indoor Stadium, Calcutta, India.

THE EVENT:
The finals of the Ruia Trophy, the Blue Riband of Indian Bridge, the 43rd National Bridge Championships.

THE TEAMS:
Formidables, five of their six players having been quarter-finalists at the 2001 Bermuda Bowl. *India Blues*, winner of six out of eight major titles in four Indian Nationals during 1998-2001.

THE PLAYERS (positions rotated for convenience of reporting):

North: K.R. Venkataraman *(Formidables)*, 'Venky' to friends, career banker, ranked world master, quarter-finalist in the 2001 Bermuda Bowl.

East: J.M. Shah *(India Blues)*, Bridge professional and international coach, ranked World Master, represented India at the 2002 Winter Olympics in Salt Lake City.

South: B. Prabhakar *(Formidables)*, holder of a doctorate in bio-medical engineering from the oldest American University, Rensellaer Polytechnic Institute, Troy, NY, ranked World Master, quarter- finalist in the 2001 Bermuda Bowl.

West: Ashok Ruia *(India Blues)*, industrialist and Bridge patron, represented India at the 2002 Winter Olympics in Salt Lake City. Nephew of the late R.R. Ruia, one of the founder Vice-Presidents of the World Bridge Federation.

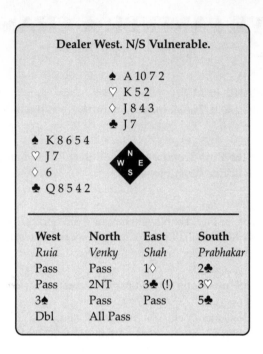

Dealer West. N/S Vulnerable.

```
                    ♠ A 10 7 2
                    ♡ K 5 2
                    ◊ J 8 4 3
                    ♣ J 7
  ♠ K 8 6 5 4            N
  ♡ J 7              W       E
  ◊ 6                   S
  ♣ Q 8 5 4 2
```

West	North	East	South
Ruia	*Venky*	*Shah*	*Prabhakar*
Pass	Pass	1◊	2♣
Pass	2NT	3♣ (!)	3♡
3♠	Pass	Pass	5♣
Dbl	All Pass		

Contract: 5♣ by East, doubled. Lead ◊6.

You, West lead the six of diamonds, partner puts up the queen which declarer wins with the ace and then plays a small club. You win with the queen on which partner discards a diamond. You now pause for thought.

West's thought process was as follows: partner seems to have bid on distributional values rather than high-card points. Even an aggressive bidder like Prabhakar would not have leaped to 5♣ without the ace of hearts. By his 3♣ bid partner surely indicated his willingness to compete in either major. Give partner Q-J of spades and K-Q of diamonds, and he should hold at least the queen of hearts for his opening bid, albeit in third position. Importantly, declarer appears to have only ten tricks, but he may embarrass partner in the red suits in the end position. What is it that C.E. Love wrote? *Attack the E in BLUE!** You therefore play the jack of hearts, not caring where the ten of hearts is because declarer cannot have his cake and eat it too – he needs the heart king entry to the table for later.

---

*BLUE: **B** = one defender **B**usy in two suits; **L** = declarer has only one **L**oser remaining; **U** = at least one threat in the **U**pper Hand (the one to the left of the squeeze victim); **E** = there will be an **E**ntry to the established threat.

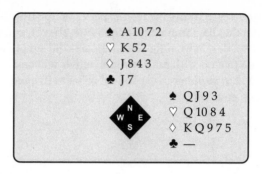

You are East now, and mentally thank partner for that heart play, because you have also started visualising the end-play. Instantly, you realise that it is going to be tricky and that you have to be careful, very careful, as to when you win the diamond king. Partner has paved the way, and it is up to you to complete a classic defence.

But this declarer is made of sterner stuff. He wins the heart jack in hand with the ace and runs A-K-10-9 of clubs extracting all of partner's trumps. With dummy to discard, the position on the last club is:

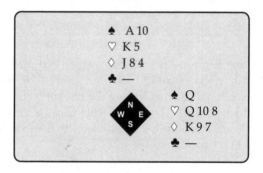

After much thought, declarer discards the five of hearts from dummy and you let go the queen of spades, confident that partner will stop spades. Declarer now plays the ten of diamonds from hand and . . . ? You have to duck now. Declarer is welcome to enter the table via the king of hearts and discard his third diamond on the ace of spades as you throw a heart or the nine of diamonds, but you are still insured. Your partner is stopping spades and when declarer comes back to hand by ruffing a spade or a diamond, you will take the last two tricks with your red suit winners.

If declarer decides to throw the ten of spades on the fifth club (instead of the heart in the diagrammed position given above), you still discard the queen of spades. Now, if the declarer plays the ten of diamonds (he still has the sixth club with him), you can either win and return a high heart or duck, but in either case you will come to two red-suit winners and defeat the contract.

The full deal:

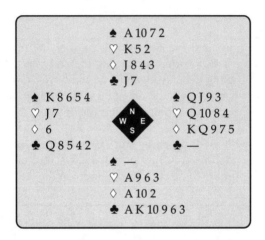

```
              ♠ A 10 7 2
              ♡ K 5 2
              ◇ J 8 4 3
              ♣ J 7
♠ K 8 6 5 4                      ♠ Q J 9 3
♡ J 7              N             ♡ Q 10 8 4
◇ 6          W         E         ◇ K Q 9 7 5
♣ Q 8 5 4 2       S             ♣ —
              ♠ —
              ♡ A 9 6 3
              ◇ A 10 2
              ♣ A K 10 9 6 3
```

If instead of that heart at Trick Three, partner had played a passive spade or a club, declarer could make his contract by rectifying the count in diamonds and then executing the red-suit squeeze on East – the delayed duck squeeze? This is possible because entries to either side of the table are available in the heart suit – remember the reference to *E* in Love's *BLUE* conditions *(page 18)*?

The defenders in the above deal representing the *India Blues* won the 64-board finals and the trophy by 2 IMPs, 129-127!

> It is so easy to make it difficult for partner. And it is not all that difficult to make it easy instead.

THE MOMENT OF TRUTH

Dealer South. E/W Vulnerable.

```
                    ♠ Q 6
                    ♡ 9 4 2
                    ◊ A 10 9 5 2
                    ♣ A 8 5

                        N
                    W       E
                        S

                    ♠ A 9 4
                    ♡ K Q J 3
                    ◊ J 6 3
                    ♣ K J 9
```

West	North	East	South
			1NT
Pass	3NT	All Pass	

Contract: 3NT by South. Lead: ♠K.

This West probably learnt his Bridge from Zia Mahmood as evidenced by his lead of the king of spades against your 3NT contract. The lead of any other suit would have given you the much needed tempo. East encourages even as you duck; West continues with the eight, won on the table as East completes his echo.

The spade lead has left you in a 'heads-he-wins-tails-you-lose' situation. If you play a heart at trick three, the winning defender will knock out your ace of spades and you can bid good-bye to the diamond suit. You seem to need five red suit winners to have any chance in this contract, but before you are able to do that, the opponents will surely establish the spade suit. You are tempted to try the club queen finesse: if it succeeds, you have regained some tempo and perhaps, only perhaps, you may be able to scrape through four red-suit winners. But you have a choice of plays available in the club suit and it seems more logical to decide on that choice later.

Another thought occurs to you. If the hearts are 3-3 and if you are able to bring home three club tricks, then you are also home. But a 3-3 break is a low percentage play. There is a glimmer of hope in the diamond suit. If RHO's holding is doubleton honour, you can make four tricks in that suit, either by finessing West or dropping the honour on the right on the second round, depending on who wins the first round. Add the proviso that West holds the ace of hearts, and you are comparatively safe.

Congratulating yourself for your good thinking, you ask for a low diamond from the table at trick three. East plays the queen and West contributes the seven, and as expected East knocks out your ace of spades with West following suit.

Before discarding from the table on the ace of spades, you put on your thinking cap again. Well, well – what is this queen of diamonds business? Is that a singleton? It does not look like a singleton, because West was unlikely to play the seven holding the four spot also. The logical corollary is that this diamond suit does not seem to be breaking favourably and, if that is so, you have to start working on the heart suit right now and that nine in dummy could well be useful.

Nor can you let go a club, and you therefore reluctantly discard a diamond from the table. You now play the king of hearts which is allowed to win, but the eight comes down from the right. You continue with the queen which West wins but there is also the welcome sight of the ten from the right. You seem to be recovering lost ground as West plays a third heart won by dummy's nine, East discarding a diamond. Just in case, thinks thou, and cash the ace of diamonds hoping to drop the king. Of course, nothing of the sort happens as West discards a club. This is the position:

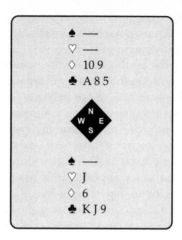

♠ —
♡ —
♢ 10 9
♣ A 8 5

N
W E
S

♠ —
♡ J
♢ 6
♣ K J 9

You have five tricks and they have collected three. The club suit has to be brought in for the contract to make. What you know now is that East started off with a 5-2-4-2 pattern and West, a 3-4-1-5 pattern. Placing the club queen with East is comparatively safer as you will go only one down even if that card is with West. An alternative approach is to pin a doubleton ten of clubs in the East hand. Fortunately, you can delay the decision of whether to drop the queen or pin the ten doubleton until after you have played a club to the king.

You ask for a small club from the table and East contributes the ten.

What is this? This deal has already driven you mad and now this blasted ten spot appears on the first round of the suit! Has East been dealt queen-ten doubleton or what? Anyway, you go up with the king, cash you heart jack on which East throws a spade, and then play the jack of clubs. Nothing worthwhile happens from the left as West simply follows with a small card. You have not succeeded in getting any further evidence.

This is the moment of reckoning. What was your original assumption? 'Drop the queen or pin the ten,' implying queen doubleton *or* ten doubleton on the right. In a very significant sense, this is an incomplete assumption. Queen doubleton includes queen-ten, whereas ten doubleton would be the ten and another card, *and* this other card is not the queen. The pinning play would necessarily involve finessing through the left. Since the ten has appeared on the first round, the

---

pinning play is superfluous now. That may not be reason enough to abandon the finesse through the left. If it were indeed true that declarer planned to play for either-queen-or-ten on the right, the finesse through the left is what he should play for now, because the ten has appeared from the right. On the other hand, what would declarer play if a small card had appeared from the right instead of that ten on the first round? The answer to that question is a matter of conjecture now, because he could play the club nine to dummy's ace hoping to drop the queen, *or* he could play the jack hoping to pin the ten. *But,* declarer had correctly deduced earlier that LHO had five clubs and RHO, two. At the point in which the jack was played, this has become three on the left and one on the right. In other words, the odds had become 3-to-1 for West to hold the queen, notwithstanding the fact that the ten had appeared from the right; East could well have played the ten from ten-small. No?

At the table, declarer asked for the ace from the table (on the play of the jack, small from West) hoping to drop the queen. *I concede that it is debatable, but to my mind it appears declarer changed his mind.*

"Able was I ere I saw Elba," Napoleon Bonaparte had said. Perhaps, this declarer was 'able' till he saw that ten spot, as the following was the actual layout:

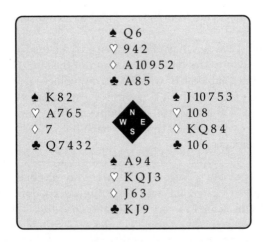

I caught up with East later and asked him: "But why . . ."

". . . the queen of diamonds? At that point in time, I believed that it was important that I let my partner know that declarer was limited to three tricks in diamonds and that I could beat the contract on my own," he replied.

When I continued: "But was that not over-communicating to declarer?" he concluded "Maybe yes. But mistakes are rarely ever realised until after we make them."

Significantly, if East had played the king instead of the queen of diamonds at Trick Three, what would any declarer discard from the table on the ace of spades? Maybe a heart or a club, but *certainly* not a diamond. If that happens, the contract is a goner!

If "this West probably learnt his Bridge from Zia," East must have learnt his card-play from Michael Rosenberg. The play of that club ten would come automatically to somebody like Rosenberg. If you think hard enough, the play is risk-less and costs nothing.

What does one do, pitted against Mr West-Zia-Mahmood and Mr East-Michael-Rosenberg?

Bid one fewer, I suppose.

These 'moments of truth' strike emphatically (Trick Three). But the real moments of truth are those which send our our opinion of ourselves for a toss (Trick Eleven).

CARDS CAN SCREAM*

B. Prabhakar is one of India's top players and indeed, one of the most popular. A ranked World Master and a quarter-finalist in the 2001 Bermuda Bowl, he holds a doctorate in bio-medical engineering from Rensellaer Polytechnic Institute, Troy, NY the oldest university in USA. Calm, and a man of very few words, he has always been an aggressive bidder and an even more aggressive player.

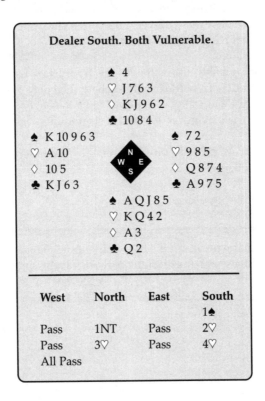

Dealer South. Both Vulnerable.

```
                    ♠ 4
                    ♡ J 7 6 3
                    ◇ K J 9 6 2
                    ♣ 10 8 4
♠ K 10 9 6 3                      ♠ 7 2
♡ A 10            N               ♡ 9 8 5
◇ 10 5        W       E           ◇ Q 8 7 4
♣ K J 6 3         S               ♣ A 9 7 5
                    ♠ A Q J 8 5
                    ♡ K Q 4 2
                    ◇ A 3
                    ♣ Q 2
```

West	North	East	South
			1♠
Pass	1NT	Pass	2♡
Pass	3♡	Pass	4♡
All Pass			

Contract: 4 ♡ by South. Lead: ♡A, then ♡10.

*First published in 2003 in *The Bridge World* under the title *The Screaming Knave*.

Moments of Truth at the Bridge Table

When I last met him in October 2002, I talked to him about my pet theme of intuition being an integral part of Bridge and pointedly asked him whether he would agree with me. He just smiled and said: "Sometimes, a particular card screams at you to be played and, intuitively you play it, postponing the logical reasoning to later." He then substantiated this, with an example *(diagram on facing page)*.

When West led the ace of trumps followed by the ten, it was obvious to Prabhakar, the declarer, that the spade suit was stacked on his left – nobody will lead trumps with a holding of ace-ten, he told me. With two club losers staring at him, the only hope seemed to lie in the diamond suit. Even then, the arithmetic just did not add up to ten. The ruffing finesse in spades and the development of the diamond suit together with the need to draw East's third trump (surely, he is the one who has it) at an appropriate time, leaves an entry short either in dummy or in hand. Since the inference is that West is long in spades, East is short there. Add the three trumps that East has, he has a total of maybe, eight cards in the minors as against a probable six in the West hand. The diamond suit is not going to come in easily.

Even as this thought process was going on in Prabhakar's mind, he heard a scream – mentally, not physically. He won the second heart in hand with the king, and realised that the jack of spades was making all sorts of noises. He played it.

West surely was not ready for the jack of spades of all cards. He considered several options for the next card he should play (if he won with the spade king now), none of which appeared attractive. For all he knew, East may have the ace of spades (why indeed should declarer play like this if he held the ace of spades?) and if that is so, he should play low. He did just that at the table, and the jack won.

Having succeeded in this little piece of camouflage, Prabhakar had to decide on another set of alternatives now. Should he play on diamonds retaining both trump entries to the table, or should he ruff two spades in dummy, the second one with the jack? That is a close call, but he could reasonably expect to take the two spade ruffs on the table, and still have time to draw East's third trump with the queen from hand, so that the spade ace will also make. That gives him two spades, five hearts and two diamonds. The diamond distribution is an unknown quantity but it probably is a little too much to hope for four diamond tricks, which is what is required if you play the other way.

After winning the jack of spades, Prabhakar ruffed a spade small, came to hand with the ace of diamonds to ruff another spade with the jack of hearts and then cashed the king of diamonds on which West played the ten. The jack of diamonds now, covered by East with the queen (he believed that dummy was dead – and who wouldn't?) and ruffed in hand with a small trump. Prabhakar now played the heart queen, extracting East's last trump, to arrive at:

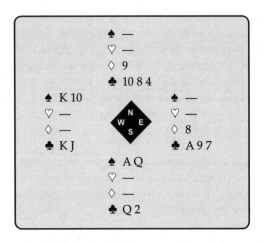

Eight tricks to declarer, one to the defence. South to play.

Although all three missing club honours were still out, there was the distinct possibility of honours crashing in the suit. If West wins the second club, declarer's ace-queen of spades will make the last two tricks. If East wins the second club, one honour would probably have already crashed, he will have to give in to either the nine of diamonds or the ten of clubs both of which will be winners!. Prabhakar played the club queen and left the choice to the defenders.

It took me a little while to recover from the daze as Prabhakar finished the story. Recovering, I asked him: "What if West had thrown the jack and kept a small club?" "If the jack had made its appearance before declarer leads to the tenth trick, then he should play a small club towards the table, not the queen," was the reply.

> A scream is a warning signal. It pays to heed, and instantly react, to that signal.

AN EAR TO THE GROUND

In my younger days, James Hadley Chase was one of my favourite writers. For sheer readability and pace of action, few could match him. And he came out with some classic titles. The above is one of them and it has eminent applicability at the Bridge table.

I watched the following layout being bid and played in four tables (in all four tables, a 15-17 no-trump was opened by East) and at every table there were particular junctures in the play where either the declarer or a defender had to demonstrate that he had an ear to the ground.

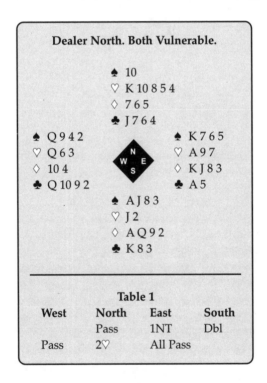

Dealer North. Both Vulnerable.

```
                    ♠ 10
                    ♡ K 10 8 5 4
                    ◇ 7 6 5
                    ♣ J 7 6 4
     ♠ Q 9 4 2              ♠ K 7 6 5
     ♡ Q 6 3          N     ♡ A 9 7
     ◇ 10 4        W     E  ◇ K J 8 3
     ♣ Q 10 9 2        S     ♣ A 5
                    ♠ A J 8 3
                    ♡ J 2
                    ◇ A Q 9 2
                    ♣ K 8 3
```

Table 1

West	North	East	South
	Pass	1NT	Dbl
Pass	2♡	All Pass	

This story is short and simple. With North as declarer, East led the ace of clubs and continued the suit. Winning on the table with the king, declarer was surprised that East-West had not competed, even though they had eight cards in spades between them. He concluded that one

---

Moments of Truth at the Bridge Table

good reason could be that the spades were 4-4 and he played precisely for that.

At trick three, he cashed the ace of spades and ruffed a spade. Next, he finessed the diamonds, ruffed another spade, re-entered the table via the ace of diamonds and ruffed the fourth spade, both defenders following all the way. The heart king became the fulfilling trick.

		Table 2	
West	**North**	**East**	**South**
	Pass	1NT	Dbl
Pass	2♡	Pass	Pass
Dbl	Pass	2♠	All Pass

The North player at Table One would have approved of this auction. But then, as they say, the play is the thing.

South led the jack of hearts covered by the queen and king, but ducked by the declarer. Taken by surprise, yours truly (kibitzing the deal) opted to sit behind East. After some thought, North played a small heart and declarer, East, put in the nine which held the trick. It was East's turn to go into a trance now. Now what, I asked myself even as he played the king of spades! Winning with the ace while North played the ten, South found that he was end-played at trick four. He tried the three of spades, daring the declarer. But this was East's day. He let the spade run to his five spot, and then played another spade towards the table. Winning on the table with the spade nine, he called for the ten of diamonds which South won with the queen. South put the declarer back on the table with the jack of spades. A second diamond to the jack followed, end-playing South once again. He did his best by ducking. East now cashed his ace of hearts, forcing a club discard from South, and the four-card ending was:

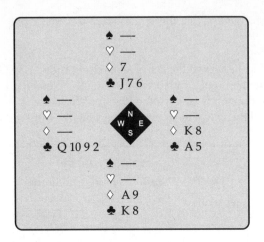

Needing two of the last four tricks, East simply cashed the ace of clubs and end-played South with a club for the third time in the deal. South had to concede a diamond trick enabling declarer to fulfil his contract.

With a wry smile, South looked askance at me. "Is there . . . ?" his sentence trailed. "No, there does not seem to be any defence when declarers read your hand like the palms of their own hands," I replied.

	Table 3		
West	**North**	**East**	**South**
	Pass	1NT	Dbl
Pass	2♡	Pass	Pass
2NT	All Pass		

South led the jack of hearts and as I sat down behind East, I wondered if this was going to be a repeat of the previous table. The queen was put up from the table, covered by the king and won by the ace. East then played a small spade to dummy's queen, dropping the ten from North.

The play now takes an interesting turn as declarer asks for the ten of diamonds from the table, which South shrewdly ducks. A second diamond is played from the table and the roof starts caving in for the declarer. South captures East's jack with his queen and plays a heart to North's ten, who plays a third diamond to complete the rout in the suit.

Down to all black cards, South tries a small club but dummy's queen wins the trick. Declarer makes one last valiant effort by calling for a small spade from the table, hoping for the only chance he has now: jack-ten doubleton with North. No such luck: as North shows out on the spade, declarer has to put up his king which South wins with the ace.

South now completes a good defence by driving out the stiff club ace and wins the last two tricks with the spade jack and the king of clubs after East has cashed his nine of hearts. Two spades, one heart, three diamonds and a club for the defence. Down two.

		Table 4		
West	**North**	**East**	**South**	
	Rajendra		*Sandeep*	
	Pass	1NT	All Pass	

For a change, I decided to kibitz the South player this time. Rajendra Gokhale and Sandeep Karmarkar are two promising players from the younger lot of Indian players. But I must say that I did not like South's pass of East's 1NT. If you lie at your first bid, you cannot give the correct picture of your hand to partner, no matter what you do later.

Bad bidding was followed by a bad lead, but the defenders recovered well at the end, although they were aided by declarer.

South led the two of diamonds, won by declarer's eight. See what happens if you bid badly? More often than not, the defence starts off with a bad lead!

At trick two, East plays a small spade to dummy's queen, dropping North's ten. Declarer, hoping no doubt for jack-ten doubleton, calls for another spade from the table only to learn the bad news as North lets go a heart. On capturing East's king of spades with his ace, South switches to the jack of hearts to the queen, king, and ace. Declarer now plays a third spade; South wins, and leads a fourth spade to dummy's nine. North has quietly discarded a second heart and a diamond on the third and fourth spades. Dummy's ten of diamonds is allowed to run to South's queen. South now takes a little time before playing a small club; the nine is put up from the table, and North refuses to cover.

Declarer had the chance to come to seven tricks in the following position:

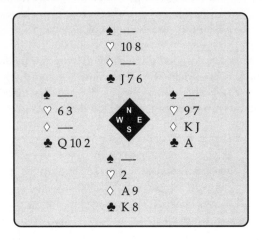

**Five tricks to declarer (East), three tricks to defence.
Dummy to play.**

Inexplicably, declarer called for a club from the table to his ace and played the jack of diamonds. South won and cashed his king of clubs squeezing declarer in the red suits. One down.

The final diagnosis
(With salutations to the greatest story-teller of them all, Arthur Hailey)

Table	Contract	Result
1	2 ♡ by North	110 to N/S
2	2 ♠ by East	110 to E/W
3	2 NT by East	200 to N/S
4	1 NT by East	100 to N/S

At table one, the moment of reckoning was the eminently reasonable assumption that spades were breaking 4-4.

At table two, the moment of reckoning was the brilliant play of the king of spades. The play ensured at least two entries to the table, as it was vital to keep all possible communication channels open.

At table three, declarer seems to have played for the nine of diamonds dropping in the third round. While South has to be complimented for that smooth duck on the first round of the suit, it is highly debatable whether North-South deserved their score of 200. As they say, opponents also contribute to your kitty.

At table four, the defenders did recover from a bad start, but it was declarer's poor judgment in the end-position that cost him the contract.

> Every call – 'pass' is definitely included – and every card has a message. To receive and correctly interpret these messages is the essence of Bridge.

BRAVE MONARCHS
STAND ALONE

Still on the subject of young Indian players, Sumit Mukherjee, 28, is to my mind the player to watch out for in the future. Working as an engineer in the Metro Railway at Calcutta, he plays with Pritish Kushari – one of India's best players – as partner. Pritish is, in fact, more than a partner to Sumit, he is a guru. I first noticed Sumit in the Indian National Master Pairs finals in January 2001, when he and Pritish led the field from the word go for twenty-one continuous rounds, only to fade away thereafter.

Sumit has more than made up since then, having won quite a few titles, and 2002 was a particularly good year for him. "Sumit is almost passionate about Bridge and he has the potential to become a truly great player if he continues the kind of hard work he is currently putting into his game," said Pritish to me. Here is Sumit Mukherjee in action.

Dealer East. Both Vulnerable.

```
            ♠ J 8 7 3
            ♡ 10 4
            ◇ J 8
            ♣ A K 10 9 5
                  N
               W     E
                  S
            ♠ A Q 9
            ♡ K J 7 3
            ◇ K 7 5 3
            ♣ 3 2
```

Contract: 3NT by South. Lead: ♣6.

East had opened the bidding with 1◊ and after North had mentioned his club suit, Sumit ended up in a very ambitious 3NT contract. East-West were playing five card majors and that probably explains West's failure to lead a diamond.

East puts up the ten on the spade lead, which is won by declarer's queen. A club is now played to dummy's nine, and won by East's queen. East now pauses for a few seconds of thought. The first idea is to put declarer back on the table with a club; that seems attractive as declarer has to play from dummy in all the other three suits and also because declarer may be forced to make three discards a wee bit early. At the same time, the diamond suit appears to offer a very good chance of tricks for the defence. When the queen of diamonds ultimately hits the table, Sumit has completed his card reading exercise: if East held A-Q-10-9 in diamonds, he would not have hesitated. The inference is that he is lacking either the ten or the nine. Winning the diamond switch with his king, Sumit finesses a second time in clubs and then runs the suit. The suit breaks 3-3 and Sumit discards a heart on the third club. On the fourth club, East lets go a heart and Sumit throws a second heart, whereas West's discard was a spade. When the last club is played from the table, this is the position:

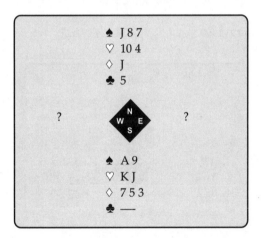

On the five of clubs, East lets go another heart. What should declarer discard now and why?

Sumit told me later: "East had opened the bidding and clearly he was having discarding problems. He had already shown, or indicated, 11 high-card points and if he also had the ace of hearts, that would add up to 15 points and he would have opened a no-trump, not a diamond. Therefore it was safe to assume that he had the queen of hearts. He had been forced to keep two spades and he was obviously holding on dearly to his diamond suit. I was almost certain that he had blanked his heart queen."

I wonder what the atmosphere at the table would have been at the time. I wonder what Pritish, his partner and dummy, would have felt at the time. I wonder what the opponents would have felt at the time.

Because the manner in which the hand had been analysed so far was nothing short of classic. If one takes a hard look at the spot cards which Sumit is holding on to, one will know what I mean.

Sumit threw the jack of hearts on the fifth club and the brave monarch stood alone. A low spade to the nine followed by the ace brought down the king from the East hand. Sumit now played the king of hearts, won by West as the pinned queen appeared from the right. Sumit claimed: "Either the ten of hearts on the table or my seven of diamonds is my ninth trick." The seven of diamonds, indeed! My, my . . .

The full layout was:

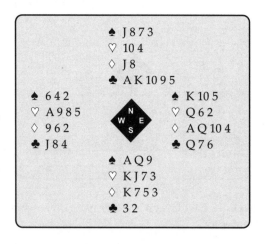

Contract: 3NT by South. Lead: ♠6.

Moments of Truth at the Bridge Table

" You are partial to diamonds, Sumit. Why did you not make a winner out of the seven of hearts?" I asked Sumit. "That probably was because the eight of diamonds was available in dummy and therefore, not with the opponents. You see, the eight of hearts was not in dummy," joked Sumit. Was he joking?

> The value, or the trick-taking capacity of a spot card, is realised only when that card actually takes a trick. More often than not, spot cards are spot-on winners.

INFORMATION, KNOWLEDGE AND WISDOM

The following story has been one of my favourites for a long time now.

Several decades ago when the thermos flask was first introduced to the Bombay markets, an office-goer was pleasantly surprised to see one in the local department stores.

"What is that?"

"It is a thermos flask, sir," replied the salesman.

"What is its use?"

"It keeps hot things hot and cold things cold for about four hours, sir."

Impressed, our man in Bombay bought one.

As our man in Bombay entered his office premises the next day early in the morning, his boss met him on the doorway.

"I see a nice little piece hanging from your shoulder. What is it, my dear fellow?" asked the boss. Whereupon our man in Bombay repeated all that the salesman had told him the previous day.

"That sounds interesting. Tell me, what is it that you have inside the flask?" asked the boss.

"Two cups of tea and one soft drink, sir" replied our man in Bombay.

That the piece is called a thermos flask is information. That it keeps hot things hot and cold things cold for about four hours is knowledge. That it can do only one thing at a time is wisdom.

Sometimes – at least occasionally, if not often – many of us behave like our man in Bombay at the Bridge table. Here is an example taken from the finals of the 43rd Indian Bridge Nationals played in December, 2001. There was no dearth of class in either the closed or open room foursomes who played out the deal. The closed room foursome was on Vu-Graph and the entire audience was aghast at the fare being meted out to them. Looking at me, the Vu-Graph commentator said; "But Jay . . ." to which I replied: "Just remember, this can happen to you one day, to me on another day. That is why Zia Mahmood once said: 'The game humbles me constantly.' While it is true that we all live to learn, sometimes we live to regret also."

Here is the deal:

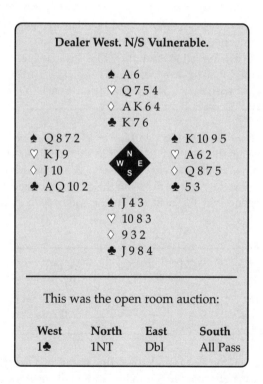

Dealer West. N/S Vulnerable.

```
              ♠ A 6
              ♡ Q 7 5 4
              ◊ A K 6 4
              ♣ K 7 6
♠ Q 8 7 2                    ♠ K 10 9 5
♡ K J 9          N           ♡ A 6 2
◊ J 10        W   E          ◊ Q 8 7 5
♣ A Q 10 2        S          ♣ 5 3
              ♠ J 4 3
              ♡ 10 8 3
              ◊ 9 3 2
              ♣ J 9 8 4
```

This was the open room auction:

West	North	East	South
1♣	1NT	Dbl	All Pass

The defence was clinical. They wrapped up five red-suit winners and four black-suit winners to hand a three-trick defeat to the declarer, and gaining for themselves a handsome 800.

The closed room auction left us, the Vu-Graph viewers, gasping for breath.

West	North	East	South
1♣	Pass (!)	1♠	Pass
2♠?			

North's pass on the first round was inexplicable. By the time the bidding came back to him, what was he going to do? What could he do? What had North learnt?

> By way of information, East-West held close to twenty high card points between them, maybe a little more.
> By way of deduction and therefore knowledge, South's hand could well be a yarborough.
> By way of wisdom . . . well, we will come back to that later.

"No matter how often I play, I will never learn the game . . . One day, I defeat a master, the next day I commit a beginner's blunder," Zia had told Ria Stalman in an interview. Here it was not the question of 'one day and the next day,' it was not even the question of one deal and the next. It happened on the next bid in the same deal, as the bidding continued:

West	North	East	South
1♣	Pass (!)	1♠	Pass
2♠	Dbl (!)	Pass	2NT (what else?)
Pass	3◇	Pass (!)	All Pass

North passed on the first round, intending to mislead everybody at the table; unfortunately, that put South in a spot in the next round. He then found that the opponents had discovered their 4-4 fit. The ego takes over from stark reality.

Given the pass on the first round – that is a *faît accompli* now - what would any Bridge player do on the second round in the light of the information and knowledge he has gained from the bidding so far?

Wisdom demands that he pass once again. It may be a conjecture, but for all North knows, East may become a little greedy and bid again.

Maybe improbable, not impossible. But what is important is that – look at the vulnerability – any bid by North other than pass, at this juncture, is certain to land him in disaster.

But horror of horrors, would you believe me when I say that this North gained 7 IMPs on the deal?

That happened because wisdom deserted East even more than it did North. Let us look at the situation from East's point of view. Your partner has opened the bidding, you have 9 HCP with Q-8-7-5 in the suit which your RHO bids at the three level, and you do not have the gumption to double?

Three Diamonds went *five* down, undoubled. A measly 500 to East as against an on-the-platter offer of 1400! Minus 7 IMPs to East, instead of plus 12 IMPs!

Lo and behold, this is Bridge, the Master Humbler.

If one looks at the whole episode more deeply, one comes across some facts represented in the form of a chart.

	Open Room East	Closed Room East
Information	Partner has 12-13 HCP.	Partner has 12-13 and four spades
Knowledge	North has 15-16 HCP, South very few	North's original pass is an attempt at deception.
Wisdom	They cannot make 1NT. Even 200 is a good score.	Asleep – the third line of the Arab proverb* on page 44

* The Arab Proverb

He who knows not, and knows not that he knows not,
is a fool; shun him

He who knows not, but knows that he knows not, will learn;
teach him.

He who knows, but knows not that he knows, is asleep;
wake him.

He who knows, and knows that he knows, is the wise man;
follow him.

> Wisdom is not merely gaining knowledge from the
> information that we gather. Acting on the knowledge
> gained, that is the acid test of wisdom.

WINNERS DISCARD WINNING CARDS

In an earlier book on Bridge *(Logic, Intuition and Instinct at the Bridge Table)* I used this quotation: "Exit cards are life-lines. A winner . . . ? Perhaps a seeming winner only." In the relevant example, a defender had to throw an established winner and retain a seemingly useless card in another suit to avoid being end-played.

The concept can be extended by the following example where a defender has to throw a winner – which gives declarer an undeserved trick – and that is the only way to defeat the contract:

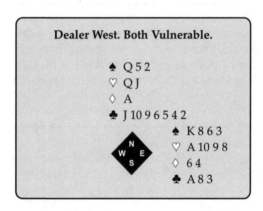

Dealer West. Both Vulnerable.

```
            ♠ Q 5 2
            ♡ Q J
            ◇ A
            ♣ J 10 9 6 5 4 2
                        ♠ K 8 6 3
                   N    ♡ A 10 9 8
                 W   E  ◇ 6 4
                   S    ♣ A 8 3
```

You are East and after two passes, you bid 1♡ (may be a four-card suit), South bids 1NT and North shoots 3NT.

West leads a third- (or fifth-) best three of hearts. You duck as dummy's jack holds. A club from dummy to declarer's queen is won by partner's king, who plays the ten of diamonds to remove dummy's only entry. Declarer is Kamal Roy who had finished tenth in the World Open Pairs at Albuquerque in 1994. After winning with the ace of diamonds, Kamal asks for the jack of clubs which you win; you then cash your ace of hearts, stripping dummy of the suit, and play a third heart to drive out the king from declarer's hand. Meanwhile, partner had discarded a diamond on the second-round club which you had won earlier.

Winning with the king of hearts, Kamal cashes the king of diamonds to which you naturally follow. There is just a suspicion of hesitation on the part of declarer but he continues with the queen, and partner follows quietly. You discard the eight of clubs and the five-card ending is illustrated below:

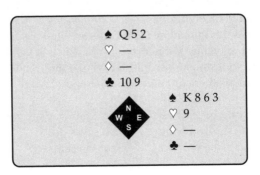

It is too late now as Kamal plays his fourth heart for the marked end-play and you are forced to open up spades. The ace of spades is definitely with the declarer and he probably has the jack of diamonds as well (partner started off with the ten, remember?). This is the full layout:

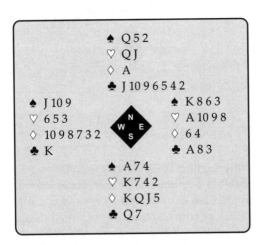

It is clear that if East had thrown the nine of hearts on the queen of diamonds, fearing the impending end-play, declarer would gain an undeserved heart trick all right, but the contract would fail by a trick as now there is only one spade trick for him and no club tricks.

There are a couple of observations, albeit after the event. As the cards lie, West can defeat the contract by switching to the jack of spades (instead of playing a diamond to knock out the ace). Another observation is that East could win the opening lead and play a spade to defeat the contract, but surely this is double dummy. The most important lesson, however, is the following.

There is an unknown quantity in the spade suit and very, very interestingly, you have a classic five-card end-position if you swap the ten and seven of spades. The position then, would be as shown below:

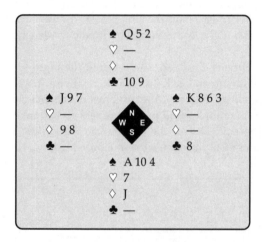

Five tricks to declarer in a 3NT contract.
Three tricks to defence. Declarer to play.

Both defenders can be trapped here. Suppose declarer cashes the red-suit winners: it is obvious that West must keep all three spades. But what East has to keep is not so obvious. Let us say that the jack of diamonds is cashed first, dummy throwing one of the two master clubs. If East discards the apparently 'useless' eight of clubs, he is in for trouble, because declarer can bring about the following three-card ending and duck a *small* spade to either defender:

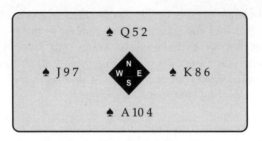

It follows, therefore, that East must retain that apparently useless club on the first red-suit winner from declarer. On the second red-suit winner, declarer must retain the club master on the table for fear that East's small club will become a master with the spade king as the entry!

When that happens, East can safely throw the eight of clubs on the second red-suit winner. The key play is to retain the 'useless' club eight because that forces declarer to retain an unreachable club winner on the table for one more round just to prevent East from establishing a winner in the suit. Indeed the *only* three-card ending in which the defenders can defeat the contract is illustrated below.

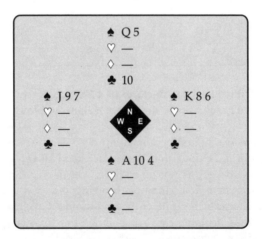

Discarding a winner to defeat a contract is, of course, excellent defence. But to postpone discarding a loser to the next trick to defeat a contract, is sheer clairvoyance.

SWINDLES CAN BE LEGAL

T he one certain thing that all of us develop (if 'develop' is the right word) as we live on, is prejudice. I am a good example. Over the years I have been prejudiced against the Pairs format with its 'tops and bottoms.' Men in the know – many of them top players – have tried to argue with and convince me that the format has its own charms, that it sharpens your defensive skills and a whole host of other things. In one discussion with a top Indian player, I remarked that all one has to do is to have a look at a few travelling score sheets which were in vogue until recently. Many of these score sheets were tell-tale: 3NT bid at nine tables, down one at all tables; 4♡ bid at two tables, made. It is not that the nine pairs who bid the no-trump game did not know of their 4-4 heart fit while bidding. The argument for bidding the no-trump game is that a majority in the field will be in 3NT trying for an overtrick. This did not jell with me because I believed that one of the greatest beauties of Bridge is to bid and arrive at the best possible contract given the twenty-six cards held by the partnership. Of course, systemic misunderstanding and judgmental errors may creep in, but they are part of the game. However, to deliberately overlook the best contract and settle for what obviously is an inferior contract because there is a possibility of a better score in the format of the event, well . . . I felt that justice was not being done to the cards themselves. "You are prejudiced," was the final verdict of the top Indian player. Maybe I am.

I should have said, maybe I was. For nearly three years now, I have been trying to overcome this prejudice by watching more pairs events. The following deal taken from one of the elimination rounds of the Indian Nationals in January 2001 helped in removing some of my prejudice.

I was at a table where Santanu Ghose (World Master and a member of the Laws Committee of the World Bridge Federation) and his partner, K.R. Venkatraman were in action (Venky later made it to the quarter-finals of the Bermuda Bowl, 2001 and the last sixteen of the World Championships, 2002).

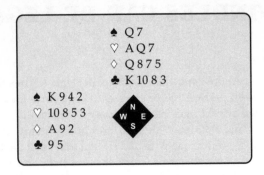

```
              ♠ Q 7
              ♡ A Q 7
              ◇ Q 8 7 5
              ♣ K 10 8 3
  ♠ K 9 4 2        N
  ♡ 10 8 5 3    W     E
  ◇ A 9 2          S
  ♣ 9 5
```

As South, the dealer, Venky had opened a 15-17 no-trump and Santanu had raised him to 3NT where the bidding had ended. I took my seat behind West as he led the two of spades.

The queen of spades is put up from the table, East contributes the six and South, the eight. Venky thinks for just a few seconds and asks for a small diamond from the table, East follows with a low one and Venky puts up the ten. West ducks.

Venky now rattles off four club tricks, East following to three of them, and then four heart tricks – the last one from hand. In great trouble with his discards, West comes down to the bare ace of diamonds, and king and another in spades. Venky exits with a diamond, forcing poor West to lead into Venky's A-J tenace in spades for a handsome twelve tricks and a top to declarer. The full deal:

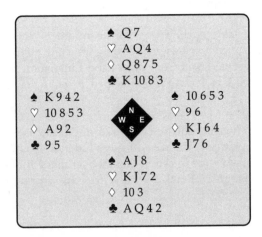

```
                  ♠ Q 7
                  ♡ A Q 4
                  ◇ Q 8 7 5
                  ♣ K 10 8 3
  ♠ K 9 4 2                    ♠ 10 6 5 3
  ♡ 10 8 5 3      N            ♡ 9 6
  ◇ A 9 2      W     E         ◇ K J 6 4
  ♣ 9 5           S            ♣ J 7 6
                  ♠ A J 8
                  ♡ K J 7 2
                  ◇ 10 3
                  ♣ A Q 4 2
```

Moments of Truth at the Bridge Table

Santanu was elated, Venky just smiled. A delightful little swindle, that.

Of course, if West takes his ace of diamonds, declarer is limited to his ten tricks. Of course, if West does not lead spades, declarer is limited to nine tricks. Of course, West must envision the end-play coming and jettison the ace of diamonds. Of course, I should shed my prejudice by watching and reporting more deals from a pairs event.

> There is a saying: "Your left hand should not know what your right hand is giving away." In Bridge, you can play in such a way that your LHO does not know what your RHO is holding.

DEFENCELESS DEFENDERS

Y ou are West, looking at ♠ 6 4   ♡ J 10 5 3   ◇ Q 8 3   ♣ A Q J 9. At Love All, partner deals and passes. South opens a 15-17 no-trump and ends up in 3NT after a Stayman enquiry reveals a four-card heart suit with South but no four cards in spades. You do not have an attractive lead, but you know that partner is holding at least four spades, so you try the six of spades.

Dealer East. None Vulnerable.

♠ K 8 5 3
♡ 9 8 2
◇ A K 4
♣ 8 6 3

♠ 6 4
♡ J 10 5 3
◇ Q 8 3
♣ A Q J 9

West	North	East	South
		Pass	1NT
Pass	2♣	Pass	2♡
Pass	2NT	Pass	3NT
All Pass			

Contract: 3NT by South. Lead: ♠6.

Dummy plays low, partner contributes the nine and declarer wins with the jack. This declarer is a thoughtful player, known for his ability to think far ahead, and this is in evidence as he leads the four of spades to dummy's king and then calls for the nine of hearts. East plays the king won by declarer's ace, who now leads the four of hearts towards dummy. You put up the ten and declarer calls for the eight from the table. Actually, you are end-played now but you do not show it as you play the eight of diamonds. Dummy's ace wins.

Declarer now demonstrates the stuff he is made of, by playing the third spade from the table to his ace as you put up a brave front by discarding a diamond. But declarer is after you as he plays a diamond to the table's king, dropping your queen. Now, the third diamond to his jack forces another discard from you. You let go the nine of clubs, knowing full well that you are facing a losing battle. Declarer cashes his heart and gives you a heart trick. You have to give him the king of clubs.

The full layout:

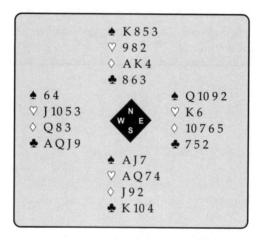

I moved on to the next table where the same deal was being played. The bidding was identical but West, after some thought, chose the queen of clubs as his opening lead.

One tempo short, I thought, as I sat behind declarer. Winning the club lead with the king, declarer played a spade to the king, finessed the spades, a diamond to the ace and then finessed in hearts. Now he cashed his ace of spades on which West let go a diamond. Hardly suppressing his smile, declarer played a diamond to dummy's king, dropping the queen, and the jack provided the ninth trick. If West had discarded a heart or a club on the ace of spades, declarer could end-play him in either suit to force a diamond return for the ninth trick.

Declarer had started off with seven top tricks which included both the major suit finesses. If it is true that two finesses are two too many, it is also equally true that neither suit broke kindly for the declarer and every card in the club suit was wrong. Still, there does not seem to be any defence to this 3NT contract.

More than three decades ago, a professor of management had told me: "There are no absolutes in right or wrong behaviour. Every behaviour is either appropriate or inappropriate." It is difficult to agree with him entirely, but at the Bridge table an analogous maxim can be suggested: cards lying wrong for you may actually turn out to be right for you, and vice versa.

> Really inspirational card-reading goes beyond logic. It comes from within.

LATIN AND BRIDGE – I

There are a couple of Latin expressions which are of great relevance to the Bridge player. One of them is *'non sequitur'*, the dictionary meaning of which is: "A conclusion that does not follow logically from the premises; a remark or an action that has no relation to what has gone before."

There are 53,644,737,765,488,792,839,237,440,000 possible ways in which the fifty-two cards can be distributed at thirteen apiece to the four players. There are similarities, some of them identical similarities, among deals which all of us have come across. From these similarities, a certain set of general rules have been formulated and these general rules keep increasing as we learn more about the game. What is mind-boggling is that the number of possible deals is a twenty-nine digit figure and when one is confronted with that kind of figure, general rules can at best be broad guidelines. They are immensely useful, no doubt, but there is always the lurking possibility of another possibility – which you and I have not yet encountered or considered – surfacing even as we bid or play.

True, algebraic impossibilities crop up during the play leading us to certain incontrovertible conclusions born out of the elimination processes: RHO has shown up with eight red cards, he therefore has precisely five black cards: no more, no less. As we move away from these algebraic certainties to, say, statistical percentages, the conclusions we reach can at best be indicative conclusions, probable to succeed. *Probable to succeed,* period. For example, the probability of a 3-2 break of five outstanding cards has been calculated at 68%. Sixty-eight out of a hundred times, the five cards in a suit will break 3-2. In other words, we move from very specific conclusions to very general probabilities.

It is these glorious uncertainties that make Bridge what it is – thank God for that. At specific moments of play at the table, players are called upon to make judgements on inadequate evidence. They have to arrive at a 'conclusion that does not follow logically from the premises,' which actually is the available evidence. *Non sequitur.* What is equally important, these situations arise more often than we bargain for.

Two examples appearing in this book come to mind. In "Disarm that Intuition," declarer's contract essentially depended on his ability to locate the club queen in a grand-slam contract, and the queen could be finessed either way. Declarer eliminates all other suits and correctly deduces that RHO is holding three clubs, and LHO two clubs and an immaterial card in the three-card ending. The elimination process has been deliberate, ostensibly, to obtain the correct count. Everything pointed to the finesse on the right, but somehow declarer did a *volte-face* for no apparent reason. He played for the doubleton queen to drop from his left, disregarding the probability percentage. That declarer was not an illogical player and he knew his probability percentages. How come, then? When I asked him much later whether there was any specific reason for his action, he replied that there was none that he could ever justify. He had arrived at a 'conclusion that did not follow logically from the premises.'

The second example, which also appears in this book (see "The Moment of Truth") is an extended corollary. Against top class defence, declarer, who is in a three no trump contract, brilliantly analyses the hand, and plays to arrive at the following five-card position:

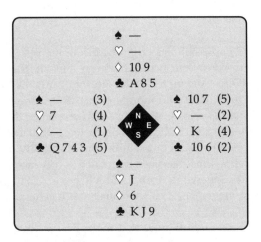

**South plays in 3NT, five tricks so far,
three tricks to the defence. Dummy to play.**

(Figures in brackets indicate the original number of cards, deduced correctly by declarer.)

To fulfil the contract, the club suit has to be brought in for three tricks. It is obvious to declarer that LHO originally held five cards in the suit, and RHO only two. Declarer chooses to delay the decision of whether to play for the queen doubleton or the ten doubleton on his right until *after* he has seen the first card from East. He calls for a low club from dummy, on which the ten appears on his right! This opens up the possibility of queen-ten doubleton on the right. What was considered before was *either* queen *or* ten on the right, and we may never know whether Q-10 on the right was considered at all. Still unable to make up his mind, declarer puts up the king, postponing the decision just a little longer, then cashes the jack of hearts (West follows; East throws a spade). The jack of clubs elicits no further information from West and declarer goes up with the ace hoping to drop the queen. Illogical? No, it is possibly another rethinking brilliantly abetted by East's ten of clubs on the first round of the suit.

Either-the-queen-or-ten on the right seemed to be the original approach. When the ten appears from the right in the first round, the queen must be on the left as per that either-or approach. Still, a re-think appears to have taken place. The explanation could well be that declarer believed that his original assumption was, well, incomplete!

> When in doubt, the mind is a monkey.

LATIN AND BRIDGE – II

To my mind, there is another Latin phrase which has great relevance to the Bridge player: *sine qua non*, the dictionary meaning of which is "an indispensable condition." Literally translated, the phrase would mean "without which not."

In the bidding, situations arise when one bidder asks (and gets a reply) whether one particular suit is 'stopped.' Then, there are the cue-bids, the 5NT-grand-slam-force, the epsilon control asking bid in the Precision Club style, and several such gadgets. In a nutshell, what these bids convey is that: "If you have this, we go ahead. Otherwise we stop." An indispensable condition, or a *sine qua non*.

But it is in the play of the cards that the concept has far greater applicability. This because, while in the bidding, the condition relates to a specific suit (or card), in the play it could well be 'one of two conditions being met, I can make the contract.' It may often be a case of 'one of two or three or four conditions being met.'

Let us look at an example in which the declarer correctly deduced during the bidding that 'an essential condition' was met, so he went ahead and bid a small slam in spades. In the play, all he needed was one of three conditions being met to bring home the contract. The deal was reported by Patrick Jourdain in the *Daily News* of the Montreal World Championships, Issue 12, and it was bid and played by Nissan Rand, partnered by Yeshayu Levit, in the Senior Teams event.

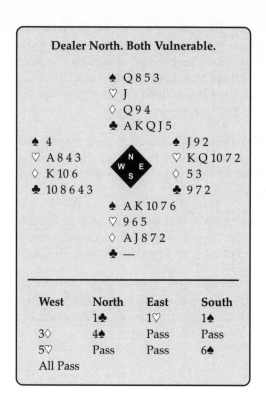

Dealer North. Both Vulnerable.

```
                    ♠ Q 8 5 3
                    ♡ J
                    ◇ Q 9 4
                    ♣ A K Q J 5
  ♠ 4                                  ♠ J 9 2
  ♡ A 8 4 3            N               ♡ K Q 10 7 2
  ◇ K 10 6          W   E              ◇ 5 3
  ♣ 10 8 6 4 3         S               ♣ 9 7 2
                    ♠ A K 10 7 6
                    ♡ 9 6 5
                    ◇ A J 8 7 2
                    ♣ —
```

West	North	East	South
	1♣	1♡	1♠
3◇	4♠	Pass	Pass
5♡	Pass	Pass	6♠
All Pass			

Contract: 6♠ by South. Lead: ♡A.

The bidding was mostly natural, with 3◇ showing a heart fit and 5♡ clearly a sacrifice bid. Nissan Rand, sitting South, brilliantly inferred that (a) the defenders' heart bids showed a combined nine cards in the suit, and hence at most a singleton with North, and (b) with partner's spade fit, a singleton in the heart suit and an opening bid which must be based on high cards in the minors, the spade slam would have much going for it.

The heart singleton in dummy was 'an indispensable condition' for the slam to succeed.

On the lead of heart ace and continuation ruffed in dummy, the sight of that dummy would have warmed any declarer. If the spades break 2-2, this slam is on a roll. Subsidiary condition number one: even if spades break 3-1, if the clubs break 4-4 the slam is on. Subsidiary

---

condition number two: even if the spades break 3-1, and clubs 5-3, it only requires the diamond finesse to succeed for the slam to make (East is the overcaller and hence more likely to hold the king of diamonds). Subsidiary condition number three: it is a sad story that on the actual layout, not one of these worked and a superbly bid slam bit the dust.

Still, there would have been no slam if the 'indispensable condition' of that heart singleton had not been met. The *sine qua non*. "Without which not." In other words, this condition is mathematical and therefore precise.

In comparison, the *non sequitur* conclusion is against all available evidence and the logic arising out of that evidence. Not that such conclusions do not succeed. They succeed less often, rather than more.

> When not in doubt, the mind is man's angelic ally.

OPPORTUNITY DOES NOT KNOCK THRICE

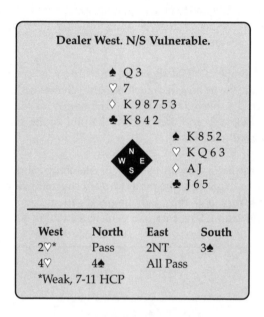

Dealer West. N/S Vulnerable.

```
                    ♠ Q 3
                    ♡ 7
                    ◊ K 9 8 7 5 3
                    ♣ K 8 4 2
                                    ♠ K 8 5 2
                              N     ♡ K Q 6 3
                          W       E ◊ A J
                              S     ♣ J 6 5
```

West	North	East	South
2♡*	Pass	2NT	3♠
4♡	4♠	All Pass	
*Weak, 7-11 HCP			

Contract: 4♠ by South. Lead: ♠4.

You are East defending 4♠ and on that inspired lead by partner declarer puts up the queen from the table, which holds the trick. Declarer is R. Rajkumar from Chennai in South India, who is known for wild bidding and excellent card-play. A heart ruff in dummy having been thwarted by the lead, declarer asks for the second spade from the table and finesses again, West discarding the nine of hearts.

Declarer now plays the queen of diamonds on which partner contributes the two indicating an odd number of cards. That gives declarer a 6-2-2-3 pattern which definitely must include the ace of clubs. It does appear that this contract is doomed because you have three red-suit winners and your spade king must make as dummy has no more spades. It appears, even more so, that the diamond jack could

---

well be a useful card and somehow the idea of dropping the jack under the queen seems to be silly.

You win the diamond queen with the ace and partner allows you to win both heart tricks with your king and queen. Is he asking for a club switch? If he is, it seems to be a little risky. Declarer might hold A-10-9 in clubs and a club switch may be dangerous. On the face of it, a third heart now seems to be the safest bet.

Rajkumar demonstrated at the table that this was not the case. He ruffed the third heart and then took the only chance he had of making the contract: he played the ten of diamonds to dummy's king, dropping East's jack, and then played the nine of the suit which East could not afford to ruff.

Declarer discarded a club on the nine of diamonds, and then ruffed a small diamond to arrive at the perfect trump-coup situation. A low club to dummy's king and repeated diamonds thereafter finished East. East's 'certain' trump king trick had vanished into thin air. The full deal:

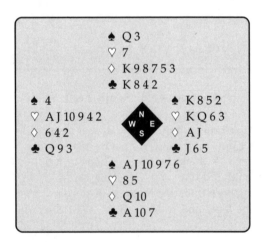

Well as declarer played, East slipped up on two occasions in spite of (a) excellent card indications by West and (b) the distinct possibility of a trump coup having become evident early on. Actually, dropping the diamond jack under the queen is not 'silly,' it is the marked play to deny that all-important entry to the table. This turned out to be Opportunity Knock No. 1 and if East had ducked the queen of diamonds, declarer was definitely going down as the spade king must make. With the club king as entry, the diamond nine can be played for a club discard, but the essential trump reduction cannot take place.

The Opportunity Knock No. 2 came when East had the chance to recover even after taking the first diamond. What is important is that East should not help in declarer's trump-reduction manoeuvre. Either a club switch or even the diamond jack after 'booking' the contract (with the diamond ace and the two hearts) will ensure that the trump reduction does not take place. Declarer cannot hide his four trumps and at some stage he has to ruff a second time and be in hand at a critical point and the spade king will have to make.

At the same time, it must be pointed out that the contract can be made anyway, as the cards lie. The key play is a low spade from the table on the opening lead! After winning the trick in hand, declarer plays the queen of diamonds – and now East can only prevent a heart ruff in dummy by sacrificing his own trump trick *or* giving an extra entry to the table with the queen of spades.

> Occasionally, safety is a misnomer. For example, in Bridge, a 'safe' play may give away a contract.

VERY MUCH ON THE CARDS

"Not improbable," says the dictionary when one looks for the exact meaning of "on the cards." To me, the layman, "not improbable" would mean "probable" although there appears to be a subtle difference between the two. And "probable" definitely means "likely."

We use cards to play the game of Bridge. Occasionally it is very much on the cards themselves – more precisely, the layout of the 52 cards – to do all the work for you and me. Here is an example:

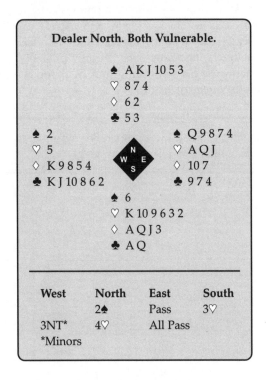

Dealer North. Both Vulnerable.

	♠ A K J 10 5 3	
	♡ 8 7 4	
	◊ 6 2	
	♣ 5 3	

♠ 2		♠ Q 9 8 7 4
♡ 5		♡ A Q J
◊ K 9 8 5 4		◊ 10 7
♣ K J 10 8 6 2		♣ 9 7 4

	♠ 6	
	♡ K 10 9 6 3 2	
	◊ A Q J 3	
	♣ A Q	

West	North	East	South
	2♠	Pass	3♡
3NT*	4♡	All Pass	
*Minors			

Contract 4♡ by South. Lead: ♠2.

Let us look at this layout as a double-dummy problem. The spade lead is won on the table with the ace and a small heart is played. East has a set of choices:

(a) East can win with the ace and continue with the queen in an effort to reduce dummy's trumps. Declarer can win, then play ace and queen of diamonds. West can win with the king, but he is stuck for a return.

He has no major-suit cards and if he plays back a club, declarer gets a free finesse in the suit, and all East can get is a second trump trick as declarer will play a low diamond to be ruffed on the table. If he plays back a diamond, declarer discards a club from the table and again East is helpless. Declarer's club queen can be ruffed in dummy and the spade king will provide a discard for the last diamond. Either way, it will be only two trumps and a diamond for the defence.

(b) East can win the heart from the table and play a diamond. This time, too, declarer can win with the diamond ace and then play the queen, and the situation is the same as (a) above.

(c) The third option for East is to play a club on winning with the heart ace. Declarer takes the club ace and plays the queen of the suit for West to win with the king. It is now West's turn to be at the crossroads. Since East should have shown three clubs, West can either give a ruff-and-discard by playing a third club, or play a diamond for a free finesse. At that point in time, West can deduce that there is no hope for the defence if declarer holds seven hearts. Also, if East had been alert at trick one, he would have shown an odd number of cards in the suit, marking declarer with a singleton. All this would suggest that declarer had probably started off with a 1-6-4-2 pattern and, at first sight, a ruff-and-discard may not be that damaging. However, on second thoughts, there is a strong argument against the ruff-and-discard play: the entry-less dummy gets an entry and the spade king will provide a discard. Even so, declarer still has a diamond loser but for all West knows East may have started with A-Q-x in hearts (the first-round ace of hearts suggests some such heart holding) in which case the entry to the table is disastrous. No, the ruff-and-discard cannot be the right defence. A diamond return, free finesse or otherwise, seems to be the marked play.

Following this line of thought, after winning with the club king West must return a low diamond to the ten and jack. Declarer will try ace and a third diamond ruff on the table, but East can over-ruff and take out dummy's last trump (if East's third trump is not higher than dummy's eight, well, tough luck). The spade king has been languishing in dummy from the beginning and it will languish till the end. And declarer has a diamond loser still and the contract will go down.

All the different approaches mentioned above were 'on the cards,' were they not? However, let us go back to the third trick. Spade led and won in dummy, and then a heart is played which East wins. Any East will go into a trance now, but at that specific juncture, is there any evidence available to switch specifically to a club, and not a diamond?

East knows that declarer started with one spade and six hearts, giving room for six minor-suit cards. This gives West eleven minor-suit cards, obviously 6-5 which conforms to his 3NT take-out bid. Further reasoning along the same lines will convince East that declarer has four diamonds and two clubs, or 3-3 in the minors, *because* West will not bid as he has with seven diamonds and four clubs.

Opposite a weak-two opening, South made a call at the three level, vulnerable, holding just 3 high-card points in the major suits. His minor suits must, therefore, be well stacked in high cards. The flip side is that partner has the missing minor-suit high cards (why did he make that 3NT take-out bid at all?). Inspired thinking on East's part will lead to the following conclusions:

(a) West is stopping at least the second round of both minors; if not, he has no business making that 3NT take-out bid.

(b) If declarer has a third club, the ruff on the table and the subsequent discard on the king of spades cannot be stopped by the defence.

(c) There is no third-round diamond ruff on the table because East can over-ruff and, if needed, scuttle dummy's third trump.

(d) As already deduced, declarer has *either* 3-3 in the minors *or* four diamonds and two clubs. No other distribution makes sense.

What are the worrisome holdings if declarer is 3-3 in the minors? If you play a club, declarer can succeed if he has the diamond ace and a third-round club winner, A-Q-J for instance, in which case a diamond will be discarded from the table on the third club, a second diamond can be ruffed on the table, and a third discarded on the king of spades. On the other hand, if declarer's third club is a loser, it can be ruffed in dummy and a diamond discarded on the king of spades, but declarer still has a diamond loser and the contract will be defeated. Even though East has only two diamonds, the same conclusion can be drawn from a diamond switch. If declarer has the club ace but his third diamond is a loser, he will lose a club trick, but if his third diamond is a winner he can discard a club from dummy, and even though East can ruff and return a trump, there is still a trump left in dummy to ruff the second club and the third club will go away on the spade king.

Similarly, with four diamonds and two clubs with declarer, a diamond switch would give away the contract if declarer holds club ace and K-Q-J or A-Q-J in his four diamonds. If not, *either* a diamond *or* a club switch will defeat the contract. To sum up, for the hands where it matters which minor suit to switch to, you have a blind guess if declarer has 3-3, but if declarer has two clubs and four diamonds, you must shift to a club. *Ergo*, you should play a club!

This last one is food for thought. If declarer has 3-3 in the minors with A-Q-x in one suit and A-Q-J or K-Q-J in the other, he might have played the stronger minor (instead of that trump at trick two) to establish his discard in time. This line will succeed as the trumps lie, but not when declarer has four diamonds as in the actual layout!

> What the eye cannot see, the mind can.

NINE IS EASIER THAN FIVE

N.P. Kabiraj, who lives in Calcutta, is an Indian National's title-holder having been a member of the Indian Railways team which won the trophy in 1997 in Bangalore. Kabiraj literally means 'king of poetry,' and I had the good fortune of spending some time with this veteran during the 2001 Calcutta Indian Nationals.

Dealer North. Both Vulnerable.

```
                    ♠ A 6 4
                    ♡ 9 7 5 2
                    ◇ Q 9 3
                    ♣ Q 10 9
  ♠ K 8 5 3                        ♠ 10 7 2
  ♡ Q 10 8 3          N            ♡ J 4
  ◇ 10            W       E        ◇ K 8 7 6 2
  ♣ A K J 4           S            ♣ 8 5 3
                    ♠ Q J 9
                    ♡ A K 6
                    ◇ A J 5 4
                    ♣ 7 6 2
```

West	North	East	South
	Pass	Pass	1NT
2♣*	2NT	Pass	3NT
All Pass			
*Landy			

Contract: 3NT by South. Lead: ♣K.

"Of course, there is poetry in Bridge. Even the arithmetic in Bridge is poetic. If you study the Law of Total Tricks, you will know what I mean. But let us look at a more fundamental problem. Who gets there first: the declarer with his nine tricks, or the defence with their five tricks? To extend the thought further, more often than not in a no-

---

Moments of Truth at the Bridge Table

trump contract, there are only twelve tricks to begin with. In such instances, it becomes a race and one player has a counter for every action another player takes."

Here is an illustrative hand played by Kabiraj in the quarter-finals of the 2001 Indian Nationals *(diagram on facing page)*.

Although the opening 1NT was 15-17, the 2NT was only a trifle ambitious. But Kabiraj in the South seat concluded that the Landy 2♣ on his left would help him in his play and therefore plumped for game. West led a high club followed by another, won on the table with the queen. A low diamond to the jack dropped the ten from the left. Suddenly, a combined 23-point 3NT had become more promising.

LHO had promised 4-4 in the majors by his bid, but still opted to lead a club. The diamond ten was an obvious singleton, giving West a 4-4-1-4 hand and that was good news because the defence could muster only three club tricks. Declarer could afford to give away a diamond trick and still manage eight tricks for himself – at least two in spades (the finesse has to work because of the Landy bid), two hearts, three diamonds and the club queen already in the bag.

Eight tricks to the declarer, four to the defence. Where would the thirteenth trick go and who would win the race?

Kabiraj mentally went through what he had learnt so far. If LHO has a 4-4-1-4 distribution, RHO must have a 3-2-5-3. The shortness in the heart suit is quite welcome as it forces West to guard both major-suits. He surely will have discarding problems on the diamonds. And if you take another look at the spade suit, your nine spot is a beautiful sight. If only West can be persuaded to cover the first spade honour from hand and if the ten of spades is with East . . . Some hands provide declarer with all sorts of chances.

So thinking, Kabiraj played the queen of spades. But this West was no mean player, he too was playing in the quarter-finals of a national tournament. He took one hard look at the queen of spades and then played a low spade unflinchingly. Plan A had to be abandoned as Kabiraj could not afford to play another spade. Declarer now embarked on Plan B by playing a low diamond to dummy's nine, West discarding a spade. East won with the king and went on a thinking spree. He had been doing his own counting and could very well surmise that there were only three club tricks to be had. He went one step ahead and realised that there could be a major-suit squeeze on his partner and that he probably had to lead a heart to break up the squeeze. He led the jack of hearts.

Kabiraj won with the ace; a diamond to the queen, a heart back to hand, and then the diamond ace finished West. When that defender chose to discard a heart and a club on the diamonds, Kabiraj could end-play him in hearts or clubs to force him to lead away from the king of spades, making the last two spades and the contract.

"How will you make the contract if East had returned a club instead of that jack of hearts? After all, that is the normal defence, isn't it? Would you not have discarding problems on the fourth club?" I asked Kabiraj.

"Then I would have adopted Plan C. I would have discarded a heart from both dummy and my hand on the fourth club and I would still have made the contract, as this would have been the position:"

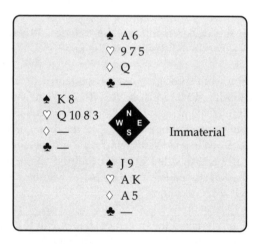

Three tricks to declarer, four to the defence. West to play.

West plays a heart which declarer wins, a diamond to the queen, a second heart to hand and then the diamond ace. What does West keep?

If he discards hearts, the nine on the table will be the ninth trick. The alternative for him is to bare the spade king, in which case the jack in declarer's hand will make. On the ace of diamonds, North has to make his discard after West and this is precisely what C.E. Love called 'the Upper hand' in BLUE (see page 18). Only the genius of a Love can convert abstract Bridge Mathematics to Bridge poems!

Very, very interestingly there does not appear to be any defence at all to this 3NT contract, as the cards lie. If a heart were the original lead, declarer can win in hand and try the spade queen. When that holds, a club must be played from hand. West can win, but cannot safely continue hearts because the nine in dummy's four-carder is a potential trick winner. If the play proceeds in this manner, the club queen will provide the entry to the table to lead the diamond queen on the first round of the suit. This also keeps East off play, denying him the opportunity to play a heart through you. Declarer also knows by now that West is short in diamonds and that there is a possibility that the ten might come down on the first or second round!

> Thirteen, an unlucky number? Any Bridge player will tell you it is the most fascinating of all numbers!

SERENDIPITY IN BRIDGE

Bhubaneswar – the chosen final abode of Lord Shiva, the Hindu God – is known as the 'temple city of India.' Located around 500 kilometres south-west of Calcutta, it is also the capital city of Orissa, home of the world famous Odissi form of dance.

I lived and worked at Bhubaneswar for around eight years during the latter half of the eighties and early nineties. It was during those years that I began to play Bridge fairly regularly at the local club and my earliest stint at writing on Bridge started there. Above all, it was at the Bhubaneswar Club that I realised that rare Bridge plays can be discovered by chance.

It was a wintry Saturday in January 1991 and we had started our rubber Bridge session fairly early in the evening. Quite a few had joined us in between and left after a rubber or two, but the original four of us continued well into the night and suddenly we realised that it was closing time for the club. As often happens on such evenings, 'one last deal,' said one of us, and what a deal it turned out to be!

With both sides vulnerable, I dealt as North and was soon looking at this hand: ♠K 8 3 ♡A J 6 4 ◇ K 8 ♣K 7 5 4. I opened a Precision 1NT, East passed, and partner bid a non-forcing Stayman 2♣. I showed my heart four-carder, partner bid 2♠ showing five cards. Systemically, I should have passed this. 'What the hell, it is the last deal.' So thinking, I made a simple raise, which was invitational. Everybody at the table was smiling now. My partner must have also thought 'what the hell, it is the last deal,' because he raised to game.

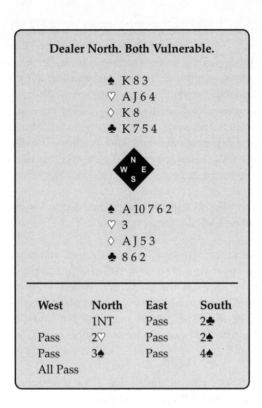

Dealer North. Both Vulnerable.

♠ K 8 3
♡ A J 6 4
◇ K 8
♣ K 7 5 4

♠ A 10 7 6 2
♡ 3
◇ A J 5 3
♣ 8 6 2

West	North	East	South
	1NT	Pass	2♣
Pass	2♡	Pass	2♠
Pass	3♠	Pass	4♠
All Pass			

Contract: 4♠ by South. Lead: ♣Q.

As the queen of clubs hit the table and I spread the hand, I asked for permission to look at my partner's hand. I must have winced because East commented: "I have heard of non-forcing Stayman and the forcing Stayman; this is the first time I have seen 'stretching Stayman' being used at the table!"

All this while, my partner, great friend and the declarer now, Sheel Dhawan, did not wince one bit. Sheel is a businessman and rarely gets the time to play serious Bridge. If he had played serious Bridge more often against better opposition, I am sure he would have become an excellent player.

The defenders rattled off three club tricks, the third one won with the ace by East who switched to the ten of diamonds. "Booked," said East, as if the others in the table did not know.

I noticed that Sheel was taking longer than he was wont to play to the
ten of diamonds. It was absolutely beyond me at that particular point
in time how he was going to avoid losing a trump trick, missing Q-J-9-
5-4. One remote possibility was queen-jack doubleton in one hand and
the diamond queen coming down on third round. Even if the diamond
queen did not come down, correct timing would allow drawing all the
outstanding trumps and using the heart ace as an entry for discarding the
fourth diamond on the established king of clubs. If indeed Sheel was
going to try for this, it was important that he won the diamond shift on
the table for the timing to be correct. But Q-J doubleton?

Probably, Sheel also thought as much. Suddenly, his body language
suggested that he had made up his mind.

He played the ace of diamonds on East's ten of diamond switch, and
next played a heart to the ace and ruffed a heart. He then played a
diamond to the king on the table, and ruffed another heart. Grim
determination showed in his face even as he played the third diamond
from hand. The queen appeared from the left and Sheel ruffed in
dummy to lead the last heart. Fortunately for him the suit broke 4-4 as
he ruffed in hand.

All very well, boldly played and all that. How is he going to avoid that
inevitable trump loser, I thought to myself.

This was the position with hand (South) to play and declarer needing
all three tricks:

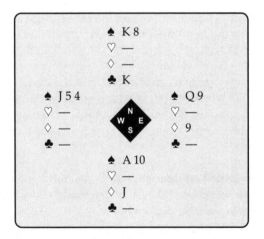

"If only the spade honours are divided *and* the nine of spades is with East . . ." said Sheel as he played the jack of diamonds. Yes!

The spade honours were indeed divided and the nine of spades was indeed with East. In the diagrammed position, West could ruff low but dummy would over-ruff with the eight and Sheel would make his last two tricks with the king and ace of trumps. If West ruffed with the jack, dummy would over-ruff with the king and declarer's ace-ten would take the last two tricks as the queen of spades is on the right. The full deal:

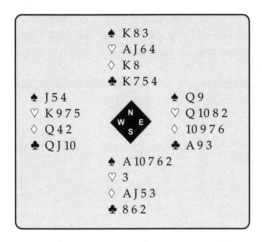

They call it the Devil's Coup, don't they?

To this day – it has been twelve years since Sheel played the hand – it puzzles me how that kind of an ending could be envisaged at the table. "I did consider the queen-jack doubleton option, but somehow it appeared far-fetched to me as I played the deal. At the same time, I did not envisage the ending as it happened, either. However, something in me told me that I should not give in easily. When I played the last heart from the table, I realised that maybe, after all . . ."

It was days later that I realised that the key play to the whole deal is to win the diamond switch in hand. The entry to table is necessary for a later heart ruff and the correct three-card end position. It was months later that I realised that the contract can be defeated if the defence opens up trumps! If it is West, it should be a low spade and if it is East,

---

it should be the queen! But I must confess that this approach by the defence (defeating the contract by playing trumps themselves) is double-dummy and almost inconceivable in normal play at the table.

But it was years later that I was able to 'connect' the play to a lovely English word, 'serendipity'. It is the faculty of making happy chance finds. Horace Walpole coined the word from the fairy tale "The Three Princes of Serendip" (Serendip is a former name for Sri Lanka) whose heroes "were always making discoveries by accident and sagacity, of things they were not in quest of."

> Bridge players should learn to use the expression 'certain loser' with caution. Losers have been known to vanish into thin air.

KIBITZER, AHOY!

"T his contract can never be made . . . " pronounced a kibitzer
after looking at all four hands – many kibitzers do not even
have the patience to work out even the fourth hand, let
alone sit quietly behind one player and, with dummy on view, work
out the declarer or defence play as the case may be.

". . . Unless the defenders fumble," continued the kibitzer, unsolicited.
A venerable foursome, all of them sixty-plus with no pretensions to
great Bridge skills, were quietly playing out the following deal in the
local club's Bridge room and it was obvious that none of them relished
the kibitzer's interference.

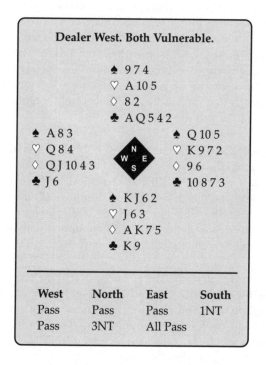

Dealer West. Both Vulnerable.

	♠ 9 7 4	
	♡ A 10 5	
	◊ 8 2	
	♣ A Q 5 4 2	
♠ A 8 3		♠ Q 10 5
♡ Q 8 4		♡ K 9 7 2
◊ Q J 10 4 3		◊ 9 6
♣ J 6		♣ 10 8 7 3
	♠ K J 6 2	
	♡ J 6 3	
	◊ A K 7 5	
	♣ K 9	

West	North	East	South
Pass	Pass	Pass	1NT
Pass	3NT	All Pass	

Contract: 3NT by South. Lead: ◊Q.

West led the queen of diamonds and as dummy came down, East got up and said "Gentlemen, I request you to allow our friend to play in my place. For a change, let me watch. Possibly, I will learn a couple of things."

"I have no problems," said the declarer, a meek old man (MOM) who probably realised that his chances of making the contract had now improved.

"How can I play, I have seen all four hands?" protested the kibitzer (KB).

"Do you know yours? Have another look, sit down and let us play," thundered West, a retired bureaucrat (RB) trying to regain some of his lost authority.

KB sat down in the East position while RB led the queen of diamonds. KB played the six as MOM won with the ace and took a little time before playing a low spade towards the nine on the table. Completely taken aback by this play, KB won with the ten and returned the nine of diamonds which held – West could not afford to overtake and continue the suit as he would be playing into declarer's K-7 tenace. So shell-shocked was KB that he had by now completely forgotten the South and West hands he had seen earlier.

'How can he ever make his contract without bringing in the club suit? Let me knock out the only side entry to the table. Ha, ha.' So thinking, KB played the two of hearts. RB made a typical 'bureaucratic' wince as he put up the queen which was won in dummy with the ace. A spade was played from the table, on which declarer played the jack. West ducked but, in no way deflected, MOM continued with a third spade as the suit broke 3-3. Winning this, it was now RB's turn to be confused.

The confusion was unnecessary as the contract had become iron-clad now. With the club suit untouched, all entries were intact. The thirteenth spade was good, the king of diamonds very much there and the second heart could not be stopped now. Two spades, two hearts, two diamonds and three clubs made a total of nine tricks, leaving the defenders with two spades, the king of hearts and the one diamond.

Did anything go wrong with the defence? That switch to the two of hearts by KB, did it not give away a second heart trick to declarer? A club shift at that point would have defeated the contract.

"With such entry problems, why did you not play on clubs early? After all, if the suit had broken 3-3, you would have had nine easy tricks," typical kibitzer language this.

"If the clubs did not behave, I would have had a loser in that suit which I did not want. I thought that in this deal, three for me and nothing for you is better than four for me and one for you."

"Seven cards in clubs with three top honours. Seven cards in spades with one top honour and a finesse to boot. You still opt to play on spades. Some logic, this." Kibitzers do not give up, in fact they are very keen to prove their point of view, or rather, prove the other person wrong.

"I agree, the way I played it, I may have lost three spades, a heart and a diamond. Logically, it can happen that way. But logically again, it can happen that clubs do not break 3-3. Something in me told me that I had to play on spades."

"Pray, may I know what that 'something in you' is?"

"InQ."

"What is InQ?"

"Intuitive Quotient."

"There is something more than this InQ, whatever that means."

"There is. Er . . . the defence sort of slipped."

I was a silent witness to all these goings-on. Game over, MOM grabbed my hand and said: "Come Jay, let us have a drink."

I was all ears as we toasted and sipped the drink.

"Years ago, I saw a lovely American movie which had Marilyn Monroe and this handsome chap with a dimpled chin and dreamy eyes . . . I forget his name . . . Robert something. The title had the word 'river' in it."

"Robert Mitchum. *River of No Return*," I ventured.

"That is it. *River of No Return*. I was reminded of that no-return business when I played that 3NT today. I did not play on the clubs early because if I had and it had failed, I felt that there was no way I could 'return' – which is another way of saying 'recover.' When the kibitzer played that fourth-best heart, I was more or less certain that if I could place the spades correctly, I was going to make this contract." MOM seemed to be thoroughly enjoying his second sip of the whisky.

"But . . . how were you so sure that the spades were going to break so kindly for you?"

"In this rat-race kind of contract, tell me which defender with ace-queen four times is going to duck that second spade? That explains why I played the third spade rather than try the clubs at that time. One more thing. The kibitzer had seen all four hands and still agreed to come in as a substitute. Tell me the name of one kibitzer in the whole world who would have agreed to come in if the clubs were indeed breaking 3-3!"

There are lessons that can be learned from the most unexpected sources.

> The great Alfred Sheinwold wrote of 'carrying the key' with you while playing a Bridge deal. It would be worth our while to clear the return path as well.

A VISUAL(ISATION) TREAT

Archie Sequeira, Management Consultant, lives and works in Bombay, and he has been in the top echelons of Indian Bridge for a number of years now. Notably, he represented the country in the 1991 Asia and Middle East Championships and won the National Master Pairs in the Indian Nationals in January 2001. On the way to the latter title, with six deals to go, Archie and his partner, Raju Arondekar, were among the leaders but they were arguing over something that had happened on the last deal. This was outside the playing area with a couple of minutes left for the next round to start. I recall walking up to them and telling them firmly – I was *Daily Bulletin* Editor – "If you want to win this, you have to get over what is past. Think ahead as to what you can do in the next six deals." I am not claiming that the pep talk contributed, but they won the title all right.

To my mind, Archie's forte at the table has been his uncanny ability to wriggle out of, and turning up trumps in, apparently hopeless contracts. He has time and again proved that these brilliancies are not flashes in the pan. I even have a feeling that he relishes being in such hopeless situations and consciously gets into them just to prove a point, perhaps.

In April 1991, the Indian Team Selection Trials were going on in Bombay. Archie and his band of young team-mates – all of them very good players – were pitted against the then all-conquering HCL team which included double international Subhash Gupta (he has played for Canada as well as India) and Jaggy Shivdasani, who had become an American Life Master in 1987 by bagging the Spingold and Reisinger double in the same year. The winning team would win the right to represent the country in the BFAME (Bridge Federation of Asia and the Middle East) Championships later that year, and which was the last step in order to qualify for the Bermuda Bowl that year. Along came this deal:

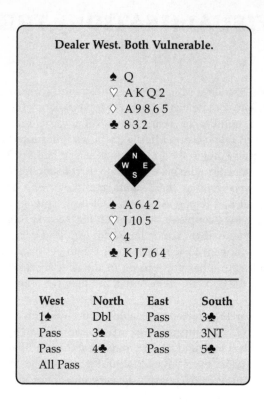

Dealer West. Both Vulnerable.

```
              ♠ Q
              ♡ A K Q 2
              ◇ A 9 8 6 5
              ♣ 8 3 2

                   N
               W       E
                   S

              ♠ A 6 4 2
              ♡ J 10 5
              ◇ 4
              ♣ K J 7 6 4
```

West	North	East	South
1♠	Dbl	Pass	3♣
Pass	3♠	Pass	3NT
Pass	4♣	Pass	5♣
All Pass			

Contract: 5♣ by South. Lead: ◇K.

Imagine for a minute that you are the declarer. You need to ruff spades in dummy: two may be easy enough, the third is dangerous because East is sure to over-ruff. You must, therefore, find a parking space for your fourth spade. And your combined club strength is so flimsy that you wish you were playing for nine tricks instead of eleven.

Archie won the lead with dummy's ace and East played the jack. Wake up call? What was this? Archie asked for a small diamond off the table to find out more and was amply rewarded when the ten appeared on his right. Naturally, he ruffed this in hand. Do you get what Archie got, at that very juncture? This was the fascinating deduction process as related by Archie himself:

- RHO has a doubleton diamond, LHO has five.

- Five spades and five diamonds leave room only for three cards in the other two suits in the West hand.

- Give West K-J in spades and K-Q in diamonds, he still would need the ace of clubs to make that opening bid.

- If the three cards in the West hand are two hearts and one club, and that one is the singleton ace, there seems to be some play for this contract.

In that all-time classic book, *Creative Visualisation,* Shakti Gawain had listed four basic steps for creative visualisation, the second of which is defined as: "Create a clear idea or picture. . . of the situation exactly as you want it."

Archelius Ronald Diego Sequeira had done just that, at the Bridge table.

At trick three, Archie played a low club from hand!

West won with his ace and Archie smiled. Who wouldn't smile?

After winning with the ace of clubs, West tried a heart which was won on the table. Spade queen to the ace, spade ruff, heart to jack, second spade ruff. Hearts cashed – East follows to all four rounds, naturally – and on the fourth heart, declarer's fourth spade goes away. Archie is in dummy with all three cards being diamonds, East has queen-ten-nine in clubs and Archie has king-jack-seven. Archie is home and elated. The full layout was:

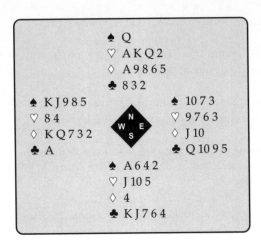

```
                    ♠ Q
                    ♡ A K Q 2
                    ◊ A 9 8 6 5
                    ♣ 8 3 2
    ♠ K J 9 8 5              ♠ 10 7 3
    ♡ 8 4           N        ♡ 9 7 6 3
    ◊ K Q 7 3 2  W   E       ◊ J 10
    ♣ A           S         ♣ Q 10 9 5
                    ♠ A 6 4 2
                    ♡ J 10 5
                    ◊ 4
                    ♣ K J 7 6 4
```

In a treatise on "Logic, Intuition and Instinct," quoted in my earlier book, *Logic, Intuition and Instinct at the Bridge Table,* Professor Mayank Dholakiya had this to say of logic: "Perhaps the cornerstone of logic is the unequivocal acknowledgement that there are a whole range of possibilities and actualities surrounding us in ceaseless motion. Every Bridge player should be consciously aware of this whole range of possibilities and actualities." Continuing on the definition of intuition, the erudite professor wrote: "The word intuition comes from the Latin *'intueri'*, meaning 'to consider, to look on.' This 'looking on' implies something deeper than simple perception and is best described as 'apperception', the ability to 'take hold' of knowledge in one glance."

Archie Sequeira and Professor Mayank Dholakiya have never met each other but both of them have the same underlying concept in mind. While the former demonstrated it at the Bridge table in 1991, the latter, who does not know Bridge, wrote about the same concept in a treatise included, of all things, in a Bridge book published in 2001.

> Willing it to happen is the first step towards making it happen.

BRILLIANTLY BEGUN, BUT . . .

MUD leads. Top-of-nothing leads. Third or fifth best. Fourth best. Intermediate honour. Rusinow leads. It goes on and on.

In the middle of a game, the play of the ace asks for attitude, and the play of the king asks for count. Many a time, partner mistakes one for the other. You and I never make a mistake. It is our partner who makes all the mistakes.

We devise, try and understand only to misunderstand later. To my mind, defence is more difficult than declarer play. But logically speaking, the former should be easier because, as the saying goes, 'Two minds are better than one.' Insofar as clarity of thinking is concerned, there is one expression that many of us use often: 'There is no doubt in my mind.' How many Bridge partnerships the world over can say with conviction, "There was never any doubt in our partnership understanding"?

Stray thoughts? Indeed they are. There is also an underlying lament.

The lament is that partners do not spend enough time together specifically with the object of improving their partnership understanding. Can anybody tell me the name of any pair in the world who have sat down and studied Kelsey's *Killing Defence* together? Forget the studying together , has any pair discussed what is contained in the book with a copy in hand? And never mind the whole book, how about twenty chapters from the book?

The deal that follows was defended by an established Indian pair who were part of the team that won the Indian Nationals in early 2001, and they were part of another team that was in the semi-finals in the next Indian Nationals. No, the objective here is not to highlight the mistake (a mistake that was the result of a misinterpretation) which was made at the table in that semi-final. The mistake ought not to have been made. But it was – so what can one do about it now, one might argue? Therein lies the catch.

Avoidance. By definition, avoidance cannot wait until after the event. There are a number of elemental understandings that a partnership must take care to develop. These 'elemental understandings' must be, absolutely and without fail, fool-proof. Ten times out of ten. A hundred times out of a hundred. For that to happen, partnerships need to spend time together and even periodically 'rehearse' their understanding. Lack of elemental understanding may lead to elementary mistakes.

Let us consider the following deal (rotated for convenience of reporting):

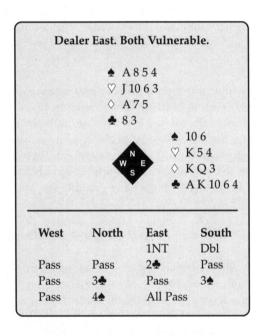

Dealer East. Both Vulnerable.

♠ A 8 5 4
♡ J 10 6 3
◇ A 7 5
♣ 8 3

♠ 10 6
♡ K 5 4
◇ K Q 3
♣ A K 10 6 4

West	North	East	South
		1NT	Dbl
Pass	Pass	2♣	Pass
Pass	3♣	Pass	3♠
Pass	4♠	All Pass	

Contract: 4♠ by South. Lead: ◇4.

You are East defending South's 4♠ contract. Partner takes a little time before leading the four of diamonds, third or fifth best; dummy plays low, you put up the queen, and declarer follows with the ten. What next? There is a good chance that you will make both your top club tricks, but where will the setting trick come from?

You need to suss out declarer's high cards and, as accurately as possible, his hand-pattern. As for the former, he surely has king-queen (maybe jack also) of spades and ace-queen of hearts. He needs a little more high-card strength for his double of 1NT and it could be any combination of jack of diamonds, queen of clubs, jack of clubs, or even any one of these cards. As regards his hand pattern, the only thing you know as of now, is that he does *not* hold four hearts. You are also not inclined to trust declarer's play of the ten of diamonds.

Surely, you must cash at least one of your club winners. You and your partner play inverted signals and as you lay down the king of clubs, declarer plays the five and partner, the deuce. Just a minute, what does that deuce indicate? Even number of cards, or encouragement? Tut, tut, you do not remember having discussed this with partner.

Assume for a moment that partner has four clubs, giving declarer two. If it were so, why did not declarer – he is an excellent player who would not let go the opportunity of a 3-3 heart break – go up with the ace of diamonds on the lead, finesse in hearts, draw three rounds of trumps ending in dummy, and then park one of his two clubs on the thirteenth heart? That way he would have ten top tricks. Maybe he has only two hearts, the ace and queen. Maybe it is a slip and he did not realise it at first.

Let us look at the probable distribution patterns in declarer's hand to see if it gets us anywhere:

(1) 4-3-4-2: Ideal for you. Declarer cannot make the contract if you cash your second club immediately. You need to play the ace, since declarer may have the queen.

(2) 4-3-2-4: You cannot beat the contract as one club is ruffed and one discarded on the long heart.

(3) 4-3-3-3: Again you cannot beat the contract as the losing club is ruffed and the losing diamond goes on the long heart. As already mentioned, declarer must have both the ace and queen of hearts. What is the position if he has only these two cards in the suit?

(4) 4-2-4-3: As partner has an odd number of clubs, he must have the queen, so you cash a club and wait for a second diamond. As partner has the club queen, you can play club ace or a low club.

(5) 4-2-3-4:This the most complex case. Declarer cannot arrange to ruff two clubs and discard his third diamond on an established heart, so he needs a club winner. If he has ♣Q-J-x-x, you have to play a diamond and hope partner has the jack of that suit. If he has ♣Q-9-x-x, then also you have to play a diamond because a passive spade or heart gives declarer the entries and timing to lead towards the club queen and cash a third heart trick. If declarer began with ♣J-x-x-x, you must not cash the club ace, and if declarer has the diamond jack, you must not play a diamond.

Partner has made a brilliant lead. It is now up to you to follow up on his good work. Unfortunately for you, you are not sure what that deuce of clubs stands for – attitude or count? Added to this confusion is the puzzle as to why declarer did not take the ace of diamonds and make the heart play (provided of course, they are 3-3).

You have made some progress in your thinking, but not much. If partner's card had indicated attitude, you would have had no problem. You would return a low club for him to win with the queen and return another diamond. But, if it was showing count, you would have to guess which of the three hand-patterns (in which both partner and declarer have an even number of clubs) declarer has. Of these three, only two are relevant, as 4-3-2-4 cannot be beaten. The choice boils down to one of two.

The full deal:

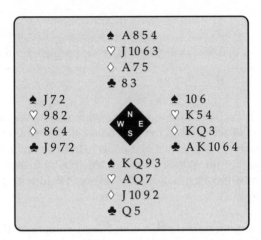

```
                    ♠ A 8 5 4
                    ♡ J 10 6 3
                    ◇ A 7 5
                    ♣ 8 3
        ♠ J 7 2                      ♠ 10 6
        ♡ 9 8 2            N         ♡ K 5 4
        ◇ 8 6 4        W     E       ◇ K Q 3
        ♣ J 9 7 2          S         ♣ A K 10 6 4
                    ♠ K Q 9 3
                    ♡ A Q 7
                    ◇ J 10 9 2
                    ♣ Q 5
```

In this chapter, many possibilities have been discussed and still at the end of it all, they all leave you and me unconvinced. Why? You and I have been going back and forth, or rather I have been taking you back and forth without any conviction. There was an underlying doubt about the meaning of a particular play by one defender. While it is true that even if East had correctly interpreted his partner's play, he still would have had to judge correctly because of the choice of plays available. The point is if it was an 'attitude' signal, there was only one play: a low card to partner's queen. If it was 'count,' East would have to make a choice out of two, not five as discussed earlier.

> Every card that you play can *help* in reducing the options
> from which partner may have to choose.

PARTNER IS MORE LOGICAL

Which partner is more logical? Your partner or your partner's partner?

K.Krishnakumar, 'KK' to his friends, who was a member of the winning team in the 42nd Indian Nationals, was a semi-finalist in the 43rd and again the 44th Indian Nationals held in December, 2002 (See "Lesser Risk, Not the Whole Story" in this book). In both the semi-finals, his team lost narrowly to the teams that ultimately won the championships.

There is something remarkable about KK's approach to the game of Bridge. In the last chapter ("Brilliantly Begun, but . . ."), he was the player in the West position who made that brilliant opening lead which had at least half a chance of defeating the contract. He and his partner lost out on the deal, but KK was more than willing to concede that the attitude-or-count signal was perhaps not fully discussed with his partner. In the deal given below, KK goes one step further and concedes that he should have gone into a deeper analysis before playing his card at trick two – this is after he had made another inspired lead.

R. Krishnan (popularly known as 'Kista' in Indian Bridge circles) was KK's partner this time around and KK, sitting West (hands rotated for convenience), was looking at ♠A 7 4 ♡A Q 9 6 4 2 ◇K 6 3 ♣5.

As dealer, KK opened a heart and the bidding proceeded: 1♡ – (Dbl) – Pass - (2◇) – 2♡ – (3♣) – Pass – (3NT) – All Pass.

Here is what KK himself had to say on his choice of opening lead:

"North seems to have a strong hand with a good club suit and a very likely four cards in spades. He is, therefore, short in the red suits. Obviously, I need to lead a heart, but which one? It is a little too much to expect partner to hold the king or jack of hearts, but I need partner to have at least one picture card to defeat this contract. With one picture card and three hearts, partner would have given me a simple

---

Moments of Truth at the Bridge Table

raise on the first round; if not on the first round, at least on the second after hearing my rebid. Which leads me to believe that declarer may have four cards in hearts, partner – I hope – two, marking dummy with a singleton. That singleton could well be an honour card."

KK led the ace of hearts and the dummy came down:

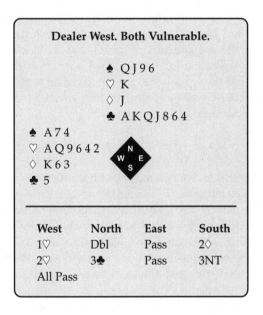

Dealer West. Both Vulnerable.

```
                      ♠ Q J 9 6
                      ♡ K
                      ◇ J
                      ♣ A K Q J 8 6 4
        ♠ A 7 4
        ♡ A Q 9 6 4 2        N
        ◇ K 6 3          W       E
        ♣ 5                  S
```

West	North	East	South
1♡	Dbl	Pass	2◇
2♡	3♣	Pass	3NT
All Pass			

Contract: 3NT by South. Lead: ♡A.

On the lead of the ace of hearts, East contributed the ten, obviously unblocking. What next?

KK had hoped for either the king of spades or the ace of diamonds being with his partner to have any chance of beating this contract. The seven-card running club suit in dummy was a dampener, because seven was one too many if not two too many. There were 30 high-card points between dummy and KK's hands and if East held one picture card, as KK had hoped for, declarer seemed to have taken a shot at game with 6, maybe 7, points only. Be that as it may, this was what KK had hoped for and there simply was not any other prospect.

But which one, the king of spades or the ace of diamonds?

The neat solution seemed to be to cash the ace of spades and watch partner's card. If he encouraged, the suit would be continued, otherwise the last resort would be to lead a low diamond, hoping that partner held a top honour in that suit. So deducing, KK played the ace of spades, and continued with the seven when partner encouraged. Kista won with the spade king and . . .

Now came East choice of return, not fully considered by KK. Which red suit and why? For all East knew, West may have started with the ace of spades, the ace and jack of hearts, and the ace and queen of diamonds. Very possible indeed. But East also knew that West was looking for either the spade king or a top diamond with him. The fact that West did not play a low spade first may have had something that was of vital importance.

The play of the ace of spades first may have been an indicator. It essentially implied that West could not afford to lose a spade *because* that probably would have given declarer his nine tricks in the form of a spade, heart queen or ace of diamonds. and the seven clubs. On the other hand, if partner had played a low spade first, he would have indicated that declarer still only had eight tricks even if the spade lost to declarer's king. This would have led East to infer that partner was holding both the heart queen and one top diamond, as West needed the other top diamond with East if the latter were missing the spade king. Even if the ace of spades evoked a no-interest card from East, West could recover and play a low diamond, hoping that the missing top honour in diamonds was with East. Thus, after a low spade first, a diamond would be the marked play because the 'top' honour may have been the king. After ace and another spade, what next? (a) If West was missing the heart queen, a diamond would be correct hoping West had the ace and the queen (b) If West was missing both top diamonds, a heart return would be correct hoping that West had the queen and the nine. That looked like a guess, but was it? Were there not pointers available? Before going into what those pointers might be, let us have a look at the full deal:

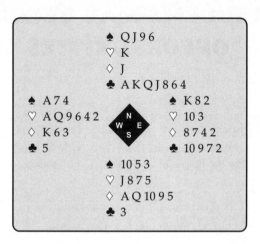

```
              ♠ Q J 9 6
              ♡ K
              ◇ J
              ♣ A K Q J 8 6 4
 ♠ A 7 4                      ♠ K 8 2
 ♡ A Q 9 6 4 2      N         ♡ 10 3
 ◇ K 6 3        W       E     ◇ 8 7 4 2
 ♣ 5                S         ♣ 10 9 7 2
              ♠ 10 5 3
              ♡ J 8 7 5
              ◇ A Q 10 9 5
              ♣ 3
```

In the post-mortem, KK conceded that a low spade first was the correct play as the cards lie. There is always a danger of an unconsidered inference by partner in situations of this kind. But . . . to my mind, there are a couple of indicators which make Kista's final deduction not that fool-proof logically:

- West had bid and rebid hearts, and still preferred to lead the ace of hearts. Why? To have a look at the dummy? This was a no-trump contract and with two other aces (East ultimately concluded that he had two other, West did not indicate that), West had chosen to lead the *ace* from a six card suit. I think one must reasonably conclude that with three aces, partner would surely lead a small card from a six-card suit of which he has the ace as well.

- The defence of any deal begins at the instant in which the lead is made. What is equally important is that a plan of defence has been made by the leader *before* the lead is made. The ace of hearts was led with that 'plan of defence' in mind. The king of hearts was smothered and *still* the leader switched to another suit. Why? It looks to me as though the presence of a tenace in the heart suit now is more plausible than the no-further-interest-in-the suit theory.

> When 'this' or 'that' is the option, a partial negative indicator on 'this' does not necessarily make 'that' the automatic right choice.

PROBLEMS MAY BECOME OPPORTUNITIES

Y ou are vulnerable, the opponents are not, and you are looking at: ♠ A Q 10 8 5 ♡ J 8 ◇ K 10 5 3 ♣ A 4. As dealer you open a spade which partner raises to two. With both opponents remaining silent, you make the help-suit trial bid of 3◇ and partner bids the game in spades.

Dealer South. N/S Vulnerable.

♠ 9 6 4
♡ Q 10 7 5 2
◇ A 8
♣ K 6 3

♠ A Q 10 8 5
♡ J 8
◇ K 10 5 3
♣ A 4

West	North	East	South
			1♠
Pass	2♠	Pass	3◇
Pass	4♠	All Pass	

Contract: 4♠ by South. Lead: ♣2.

The lead has been explained as third/fifth best. How do you proceed?

You would probably be able to ruff one diamond in dummy. If the trumps break 3-2 and the honours are divided, you have four spades,

---

four minor-suit tricks, and the diamond ruff on the table; that adds up to only nine. One chance is for the diamond Q-J-x to come down, making the ten a master. Another is for the third heart to make – there is a problem here, however, in that you have to play spades twice from dummy, it will take two rounds to knock out the top heart honours, hearts may not break 3-3 which means you have to draw all trumps before cashing your established heart and you need an entry to the table for doing that.

Since you have to play spades twice from the table, you win the opening lead in dummy and play a small spade. East puts in the deuce and you play the eight expecting it to lose. West surprises you by discarding a low diamond. Problem compounded. What is it that they say? Yes, do not look at a problem as a problem, but look at it as an opportunity.

So, East has five spades. What are his other eight cards? As a first step towards discovering that, you play the eight of hearts, West hops up with the king and leads another club on which East plays the jack, and you win in hand. You continue with the jack of hearts, but this time East wins with the ace and shoots back the queen of diamonds. Is that diamond queen a singleton, you wonder?

Even as you wonder, you ponder. That lead of the two of clubs was announced as third/fifth best. If West had three clubs, East must have five. East has already shown up with five spades, two hearts and the queen of diamonds. If you add the five clubs, he has no room for any more red cards. Which means you have only one ready-made red-suit winner *and* East will have enough clubs as exit cards. You cannot afford that and since you cannot afford that, you hope for something better.

Conclusion 1
You have to play for East to hold three clubs.

If East has three clubs, there is room for two more cards in his hand. He must, therefore, have started with four hearts and one diamond, or three hearts and two diamonds, or two hearts and three diamonds – at least that is how you are narrowing down the alternatives. If East holds four hearts, it is good news in one sense but worse news in another. You can take the diamond queen return on the table, cash two hearts to which East follows, whilst you discard two diamonds from hand. If you play the fifth heart now, East will ruff small which you have to over-ruff, and arrive at:

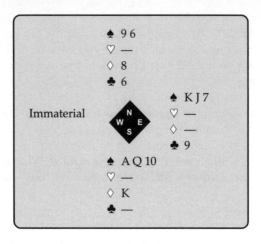

You are in hand – there is no way you can make three out of these four cards. Whether you play the diamond king or the spade, East can win and has no problems with his return since, with dummy's six of clubs in in full view, he *knows* he has a club winner.

If you had chosen to cash only two hearts and played dummy's third club (instead of that fifth heart) and ruffed it in hand, the position would have been:

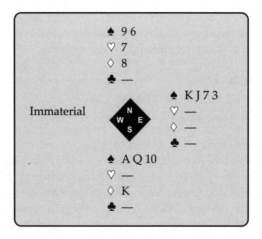

The position here is slightly different, but only slightly. The clinching point is that East has four trumps and you have only three. With the lead in your hand, whatever you play, East must make two spade tricks. Again, down one.

Conclusion 2
You have to play for East to hold at least two diamonds.

You still have work to do, because East may have two hearts and three diamonds, or three hearts and two diamonds. Let us assume it is the former. You win the diamond queen in hand and play another diamond to dummy's ace to which East follows. You can now play either black suit and succeed. For example, ruff a club, ruff a diamond, finesse in trumps and exit with the ten of diamonds.

Which brings us to the last possibility of East holding three hearts and two diamonds, which was the actual layout. This was the position when the queen of diamonds was played:

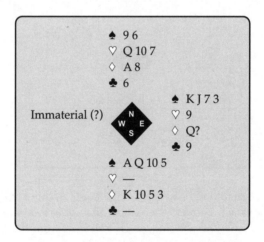

```
              ♠ 9 6
              ♡ Q 10 7
              ◇ A 8
              ♣ 6
                          ♠ K J 7 3
Immaterial (?)            ♡ 9
              N           ◇ Q?
            W   E         ♣ 9
              S
              ♠ A Q 10 5
              ♡ —
              ◇ K 10 5 3
              ♣ —
```

Three tricks to declarer in his 4♠ contract.
Two tricks to defence. East plays the ◇Q.

It was again Archie Sequeira (see "A Visual[isation] Treat") who was the declarer, and sitting East was a top Indian player.

Archie took the queen of diamonds in hand and played a diamond to the ace on the table and down came the jack of diamonds from the East hand. An unexpected bonus? Yes, indeed, but for an altogether unexpected reason as we shall see later. Dummy's queen of hearts was cashed, to which both defenders followed while Archie discarded a diamond. The fourth heart was played from dummy, East ruffed with the three and Archie had to over-ruff, which he did with . . . the ten. Archie now played the established ten of diamonds, discarding the club from the table. Since discarding would not do him any good, East ruffed the ten of diamonds and exited with his third club, which Archie ruffed with the five in hand and over-ruffed with the nine in dummy. Archie was right where he wanted to be, and took the last two tricks with the ace and queen of spades.

This was the full deal:

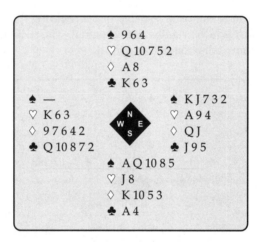

If the jack of diamonds had been with West, Archie could not have made his contract, because the critical play was the winning ten of diamonds to pave the way for the club discard from the table, at the same time forcing East to ruff with his third trump. Poor East was now reduced to one trump fewer than declarer's, and could only play his club for that vital over-ruff in dummy with the nine.

Some tricks are like hidden treasures. You may have to keep on digging to bring them to the surface.

THAT PARTNER OF MINE . . . !

"That partner of mine . . ." began the grand old man, a veteran of more than four decades of tournament Bridge, who has had many successes in good, competitive fields. He has also a seven-year itch, as he religiously changes his partner every seven years. The current partner is a good thirty years younger than the grand old man.

"That partner of mine, do you know him, Jay?"

"Yes, I know him well."

"He has this habit of putting me in almost unmakeable contracts. Only two days ago he put me in a four spades contract missing all the three top honours in trumps and with just eight trumps between us."

"Did you make the contract?"

"I did make the contract but you have no idea what I went through."

"Tell me."

He told me and it was clear that he had played the hand well. Nothing outstanding, but just good deductions after a normal elimination process.

"That was nicely played," I said, and added, "but you must admit that you get the opportunity to play such interesting hands only if you bid them. Isn't that so?"

"I agree there. But there ought to be some comfort level while playing a hand."

"What is this 'comfort level' business? I am not sure I understand."

"Let me explain. I had opened one spade holding jack-ten-nine to five and 16 high-card points. He had ten points and he forced me on the first round; I tried two no-trumps implying a bad spade suit, but he jumped to four spades with just three trumps to the eight. In his place, I would have responded one no-trump or even two spades on the first round, and we definitely would have signed off without reaching game."

"Sixteen plus ten makes twenty-six and a trump fit of eight cards is, to my mind, good enough for a major game. And your two no-trumps, albeit after a forcing response, surely invited game. Isn't that so?"

"But three to the eight? I definitely expected an honour with him."

"So could he. He had no means of knowing that you had a jack-high suit."

"The system, as we play it, allows me to open any five-card major. The system, as we play it, does not allow a jump raise to game with three-card support headed by the eight!"

"What would you have done if he had just bid three spades over your two no-trumps?"

"I reckon I would have raised to four."

"So long as the final contract is the same, does it matter who bids it?"

"It does. If he had slightly undervalued his hand in the first instance by bidding one no-trump and then supported spades, it would have given me a warning signal and my measly spade suit is additional reason for me to stop below game."

He probably had something there. Let us have a look at the two hands and see how the play went:

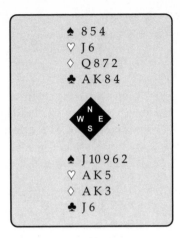

♠ 8 5 4
♡ J 6
◇ Q 8 7 2
♣ A K 8 4

N
W E
S

♠ J 10 9 6 2
♡ A K 5
◇ A K 3
♣ J 6

The defence began brilliantly as West cashed the ace of spades and continued the suit for East to win the next two tricks with the other two top honours, effectively drawing all of dummy's trumps and preventing the heart ruff. East then switched to the ten of hearts.

Without even having a chance to have a go at the contract, the grand old man found that he has been 'booked'. His chance number one was to hope for a 3-3 diamond break. His chance number two was to find West with at least 4-4 in the minors – and, fortunately for him, chances one and two could be combined. Chance number three was the double squeeze with hearts as the common suit. This chance would imply that one defender stopped hearts and a minor, the other hearts and the other minor. Unfortunately for the declarer, that heart switch had taken away the possibility of the 'either minor with either defender' option. If the heart had not been played, declarer would have ruffed the third club, discarded one heart on his fifth spade and still would have a heart on the table to re-enter his hand, to arrive at this superb position, with dummy to play:

```
              ♠ —
              ♡ J
              ◇ 8
              ♣ 8

Two hearts and    N        Two hearts and
a minor winner  W   E      a minor winner
                  S

              ♠ —
              ♡ A K 5
              ◇ —
              ♣ —
```

Two hearts and a minor winner

Two hearts and a minor winner

Since East made that deadly switch to a heart after cashing the third spade – effectively scuttling a free heart discard from the table – the above three-card position is unattainable. The double squeeze with West holding diamonds and East clubs, with hearts as the common suit, is still possible. In the four-card ending, West is reduced to a single heart by the play of the last trump and then the same fate befalls East on the next trick when declarer crosses to dummy's queen of diamonds. Rather than get into any further complicated thinking, the grand old man felt that a combination of chance numbers one and two would surely be a good chance indeed. He plumped for that combination of chances, and was rewarded when West turned up with 4-4 in the minors and had no answer to the minor-suit squeeze on him. "I enjoyed playing the deal, of course. However, I still maintain that success in one deal is no justification for system indiscipline," said the grand old man.

Just then, the younger partner joined us and asked whether it was the same 4♠ deal which was being discussed. When told yes, he said: "With any other partner, I would have been more cautious and we may not have bid game." The old man smiled at the young man's implied compliment, even as I admired the young man's diplomacy.

Partner's compliments make partnerships complementary.

LUCK CAN BE CRUEL

A couple of years ago, during a major Indian tournament, a twenty-three-year-old promising Bridge talent – let us call him Chirag – sought me out and explained in good detail what had happened to him in a deal that he played just that morning. There was an air of injured pride in what he was relating. With opponents silent throughout, Chirag had opened a Precision 1♣ with 19 HCP, partner responded a negative 1◊, Chirag rebid 2NT which partner raised to three. A fourth best seven of hearts was the opening lead.

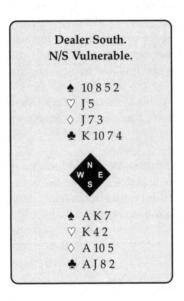

Dealer South.
N/S Vulnerable.

♠ 10 8 5 2
♡ J 5
◊ J 7 3
♣ K 10 7 4

♠ A K 7
♡ K 4 2
◊ A 10 5
♣ A J 8 2

Contract: 3NT by South. Lead: ♡7.

Chirag had hopefully put up the jack from dummy at trick one, but East won with the ace and shot back the nine. West overtook with the queen and played the eight. The first of the problems was to find a discard from the table on this, but Chirag ultimately decided on a low diamond, and won in hand with the king as East followed suit. The deduction was that hearts were 5-3.

The club suit had to be brought in for all four tricks and the safety play of finessing through West had to be made. Even if these conditions were met, there were only eight tricks *unless* East held both missing diamond honours. Chirag also saw a flicker of opportunity in the spade suit. If the suit broke 3-3 and the queen was with East, declarer could make an avoidance play in such a way that East did not jettison the queen under one of the top honours. Of course, there was an additional proviso here in that the declarer needed three entries to the table and they all had to come from the club suit only. "Beginner's luck you might call it, but I decided to play for this latter option," said Chirag to me.

On winning with the king of hearts, Chirag played the eight of clubs to dummy's ten, both opponents following with low cards. A low spade from dummy fetched the four from East, the ace from hand, and the three from West. Chirag now played the jack of clubs to dummy's king, East following. (Note that it would be a mistake for declarer to cash the club ace before playing the jack of clubs, because if East had started with a doubleton club, he could discard a spade on the third club). A second low spade from dummy followed, on which East put in the jack. What now?

"I started off with an assumption and I have no reason to change that assumption now," believed Chirag as he won with the king and confidently played a third round of spades. The suit broke 3-3 and East had the queen, so Chirag was home.

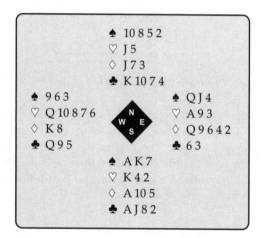

I warmly complimented Chirag, but mildly suggested that he had been lucky.

"Why lucky, Mr Jayaram? Do you know what happened at the other table? The declarer cashed ace and king of spades at tricks four and five. Poor East could do nothing about it with that dummy staring at him. My jettison-avoidance play came to nothing."

"This game is for never-say-die brave hearts. As you spend more years playing the game, you will learn to become phlegmatic about this luck factor. If anybody tells you that there is no luck in duplicate Bridge, ask him to go jump in the nearest river after checking up with him that he can swim. Yes, to a very, very large extent the luck factor has been eliminated. But, no sir, it has not been eliminated altogether. It never will be," I advised the young man.

> In the long run, luck sort of evens out.

NOT YOUR DAY

You are West, vulnerable against non-vulnerable opponents. Your RHO, the dealer, opens a natural 1♣, and looking at ♠A K J 8 5 2 ♡K 10 6 5 2 ◇6 ♣J, you overcall with a simple 1♠. The bidding then proceeds thus: (1♣) – 1♠ – (2♣) – 2♠ – (3♣) – ? What do you bid now? Do you, or do you not, show your heart suit? The advantage in showing the suit is that partner will be better informed. The disadvantage is that the opponents will know more than they need to know. How about 3♠ 'to see what develops'? The risk in making that bid is that it may well be passed out and you may miss a cold game contract. You must not lose sight of the fact that you are holding a distributional powerhouse *and* partner has indicated support for your six-card suit.

There is a third dimension. It is clear from the bidding that, between the opener and you, the combined high-card strength is of the order of at least 65% and the respective partners are bidding for the purpose of competing only. In other words, this is one of those deals in which the battle lines are drawn between the opener and you. It is also true that it may turn out to be either of the partners – not the opener, not you – who may have to take the final decision before the auction is closed. That final decision would essentially depend on how much information that player has about his partner's (yours or the opener's) hand.

It is a close call but ultimately you decide that 4♠ is not inappropriate, so you make that call. After two passes, opener comes in with 5♣! Obviously he believes that you can make 4♠. Is there something in his belief from which you can draw an inference? Is he trying to push you to 5♠?

You seem to have landed yourself in a larger difficulty now. Hindsight tells you now that if you had bid 3♡ over 3♣ 'to see what develops,' you would have been better off. Further bidding by the others would have given you fuller information. You would certainly not have stopped short of game and, most importantly, your partner would have been better informed. But that is past now, and all you can logically do at this point is to pass – the 'forcing pass', as it is fashionably called. In the common parlance, the synonym for 'forcing pass' is 'passing the buck."

Let us turn our attention to East now. He is looking at the following cards: ♠Q 10 3 ♡A J 8 3 ◊J 10 9 7 ♣6 4. What he knows is that his partner has good spades with about 13 high-card points. With the hand he is holding, East just cannot see eleven tricks in spades, nor can he see 5♣ making. 'Probably the bidding will be the same at the other table,' is the eminently reasonable thought that crosses East's mind. He has, therefore, only one option. He doubles.

Against 5♣ doubled, you lead the ace of spades and dummy comes down with ♠7 6 ♡Q 9 4 ◊A Q 8 3 ♣8 7 5 2. You cash your second spade honour also, and then switch to the singleton diamond. Declarer puts up the ace from the table and partner plays the jack. This is followed by two rounds of trumps, to both of which partner follows. Declarer now plays a low heart towards the table and it is over to you again.

Today does not seem to be your day as, for the third time in this deal, you are at the crossroads. The thought that occurs to you is that this declarer is trying to hoodwink you. You know by now that the declarer holds the ace, king and queen in clubs and the diamond king, but that adds up to 12 high-card points only. Is he holding the ace of hearts as well? You reason out that he may well have a 2-2-3-6 hand pattern and if he has the ace of hearts also, you have to act here and now by taking your king of hearts. If you do not, horror of horrors, the declarer may well end up making the contract! And if that does happen, your wife will have a great story to tell your grandson: "This grandfather of yours has a habit of not taking what is offered to him on a platter. Once at the Bridge table, the declarer offered him the setting trick and your grandpa did not take it!" Your thinking does not stop at that. You go to the extent of mentally patting yourself on the back for having succeeded in pushing this declarer to the five level and collecting 100 – if the layout is as envisaged, four spades cannot make because of the two losers in hearts and the two minor suit aces!

You go up with the king of hearts making sure of that 100 – and no story-to-the-grandson.

Having won with the king, you continue with another heart which declarer ruffs. He then runs the club suit squeezing your partner in the red suits – the heart queen on the table is a threat against your partner's ace – ending up with ten tricks. You have got your 100 points all right.

Deal over, you recollect the full fifty-two-card layout and go through an 'agonising reappraisal' as John Foster Dulles once said. You realise that 4♠ is cold and that five is makeable if the heart finesse is taken correctly. You find out later that your opponents did go to 5♠ and guessed the heart position correctly to collect 650.

All those clever-after-the-event fellows will try to tell you that you should have shown your hearts, that you should have realised that your partner would not have made two bids holding four glorious points (without the ace of hearts), that you should not have taken the heart king in which case you would have collected 300 – just grin and bear all those comments. No purpose will be served by telling them that you actually considered bidding 3♡ and that your forcing pass was a mandate to partner to either bid 5♠ if he had a better hand (vulnerability odds), or double if he had a poor hand. You resign yourself to just this thought: today is not your day!

The deal occurred in one of India's matches during the Bridge Championship that preceded the 2002 Commonwealth Games in Manchester. The declarer was Sundar Ram of the Sundar-Sridhar combination, easily one of India's top pairs. They have been partners for nearly twenty years and it is my considered belief that they will one day become a world-class pair.

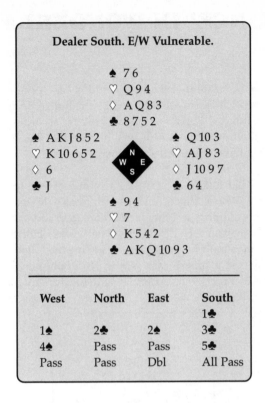

Dealer South. E/W Vulnerable.

```
                ♠ 7 6
                ♡ Q 9 4
                ◊ A Q 8 3
                ♣ 8 7 5 2
♠ A K J 8 5 2                   ♠ Q 10 3
♡ K 10 6 5 2        N           ♡ A J 8 3
◊ 6              W     E         ◊ J 10 9 7
♣ J                 S           ♣ 6 4
                ♠ 9 4
                ♡ 7
                ◊ K 5 4 2
                ♣ A K Q 10 9 3
```

West	North	East	South
			1♣
1♠	2♣	2♠	3♣
4♠	Pass	Pass	5♣
Pass	Pass	Dbl	All Pass

Contract: 5♣ by South, doubled. Lead: ♠A.

Two thoughts occur to me. They may not be great lessons, but they are
worth a mention nevertheless.

One: at the table at which 5♠ was bid and made, the heart queen was
successfully finessed. Perhaps – I concede that it is only 'perhaps' – in
an auction where one player keeps on bidding and rebidding one suit
only, it behoves to place him with a singleton somewhere. Not fail-
proof, of course, but a good pointer nevertheless.

Two . . . well, see below:

> Today's cleverness-after-the-event may well become
> tomorrow's before-the-event guideline.

'PRINCE' IN WONDERLAND

Literally translated, Rajkumar would mean 'prince.' Popularly and fondly nicknamed 'Kibitzer,' by the Indian Bridge fraternity, Chennai-based Rajkumar is a wild bidder according to many of us, the so-called puritans. It is as well he bids like that. If he did not, we would not have witnessed some amazing plays.

"Rajkumar? That fellow . . . " said Avinash Gokhale to me recently (Avinash is a World Master and a semi-finalist in the 1988 World Championships amongst other achievements), and Avinash's eyes conveyed the rest to me. P. Sridhar – the world of Bridge will hear more of this man in the coming years – sent me the following deal and said: "Rajumar is a superb card player. No doubt he often gets into adventurous contracts, but he dazzles with his dummy play."

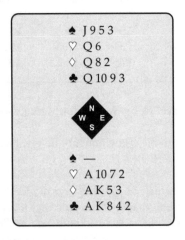

```
              ♠ J 9 5 3
              ♡ Q 6
              ◊ Q 8 2
              ♣ Q 10 9 3
                   N
                W     E
                   S
              ♠ —
              ♡ A 10 7 2
              ◊ A K 5 3
              ♣ A K 8 4 2
```

West deals and opens a 15-17 no-trump. Over to you, South. What is your final contract?

Some number of clubs, obviously. Six? While the opening bid has clearly marked the king of hearts on your left, you should be able to ruff the fourth heart on the table (also, the jack of hearts might come down on the third round). Additionally, the diamond suit has to break 3-3, *or* clubs might break 2-2 *or* West might hold four diamonds and three clubs.

No sir! Methinks 5♣ would be safer.

Rajkumar bid 7♣ clubs! Do not ask me how he got there, I just do not know. What I do know is that he reached seven and *made* seven.

West led the ace of spades which Rajkumar ruffed low. A low club from hand to the nine on the table held. A second spade from the table, ruffed high in hand, fetched the king from the left. Another low club to dummy's ten and RHO discarded a small spade. The third spade from the table, again ruffed with a high honour, fetched the queen from the left. Incidentally, this was the last trump in declarer's hand. Rajkumar has always liked the name 'Vienna', so he cashed the ace of hearts and then played a low diamond to dummy's queen. He now played the queen of clubs and then the fourth club from the table to arrive at:

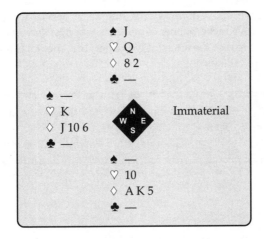

The master jack of spades is played and the ten of hearts from hand is discarded. West has no safe discard and the 'prince' has made his grand slam! The full layout:

A dummy reversal. A non-material finesse. A Vienna Coup. What do you call this? A Knickerbocker Glory? It is when we are witness to such plays that we realise the amazingly exhilarating mental levels to which this game can take us.

> "What lies behind us and what lies before us are tiny matters, compared to what lies within us."
>
> *Oliver Wendell Holmes*

THE CRISS-CROSSED LADY

B elieve me, I am not a male chauvinistic pig. Please believe me. You don't believe me? Read on.

As a teenager, I used to accompany my dad to the club and watch him play Bridge. It was there that I picked up my early Bridge lessons. One day, one of my dad's friends gave me the book *The Bridge Immortals* and told me that I would enjoy reading it. The book was an old edition, complete with photographs on art paper. Today – it has been decades now – I can visualise only two of those photographs. A face that had determination written all over it – the name was Rixi Markus. Another face looked so kindly that I wondered how she managed to hold her own in what was essentially considered to be a man's world (pray, where is the logic in that?) – the name was Fritzi Gordon. As against this, the only male face (from the world of Bridge) that I can visualise is Alfred Sheinwold's. That is possibly because I bought six of his puzzle books and each one of them had his photograph on the back cover.

Unconvinced that I am not a male chauvinistic pig? Consider this: the book which you are now reading has been edited by Elena Jeronimidis. Do you think she would have allowed me to get away with it if I had written anything against lady Bridge players? Not even in the wildest dreams of my disordered head would I have attempted such a sacrilege.

You still don't believe me? Read on.

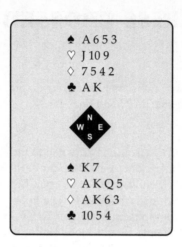

♠ A 6 5 3
♡ J 10 9
◇ 7 5 4 2
♣ A K

♠ K 7
♡ A K Q 5
◇ A K 6 3
♣ 10 5 4

Contract: 6 ♡ by South. Lead: ◇8.

The declarer is a brilliant young player, P. Sridhar who, many in India believe, will reach high levels in the world of Bridge very soon. On his right is a major from the Army, the usual smartly-attired one with a bushy moustache. On Sridhar's left is the major's wife, also the usual one trying to look and act more sophisticated than sophistication itself.

With both opponents remaining silent throughout, Sridhar and partner bid to 6◇ after having discovered the good high card strength and the 4-4 fit in diamonds. Bored at the proceedings till the 6◇ bid was made, the lady *thunders* a double. Sridhar is taken aback, but recovers in time to run to 6 ♡.

Obviously disappointed, the lady leads the eight of diamonds and Bushy Moustache ruffs. Now Sridhar knew why she looked disappointed; she had three trump winners in a diamond contract. After ruffing the first trick – rather triumphantly, after all it is the first trick in a contract bid and played by a young man who has represented the country in the Commonwealth Games at Manchester – Bushy Moustache switches to the queen of spades. Sridhar wins in hand, plays a low spade to dummy's ace, and then ruffs a spade high in hand. Five of trumps to dummy's jack, and then dummy's last spade is again ruffed high in hand. The last top trump honours from hand are now cashed, to which both defenders follow. A club to dummy's ace brings Sridhar to the following five-card position:

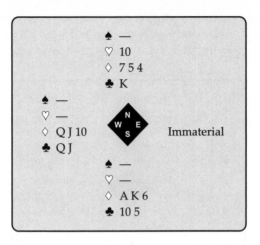

The ten of hearts draws the last trump from East, Sridhar throws the six of diamonds, and the lady crosses her legs. First the right one over the left, then the left over the right and finally back to the right over the left. She finally lets go the queen of clubs. Not to be undone, Sridhar now cashes the king of clubs – that brings down the jack, of course. The ace and king of diamonds and the established ten of clubs provide the last three tricks to the declarer. It would not have helped the lady to throw a diamond (as Sridhar did) on the ten of hearts; in that case a diamond would be played from the table for the ace and king of that suit to be cashed, and the club king would provide the entry for the established seven of diamonds. Criss-cross!

"Why did you have to double 6◊?" asks Bushy Moustache, not unreasonably. Not one to let go an opportunity like this, chivalrous Sridhar comes to the rescue of the lady by suggesting to Bushy Moustache "If you had switched to a club at trick two, my lines of communications are broken and I cannot make this contract." Visibly thankful, the lady says: "See, I led the smallest of my diamonds, the eight, as a suit preference signal. I wish you would follow my lead once in a while."

"Also," continues Sridhar, "the contract cannot be made if the opening lead is not ruffed." But Sridhar is completely swept off the ground when the lady turns to him and asks: "What is that end-play called? It is on the tip of my tongue, but I cannot recall it straightaway."

Recovering just in time, Sridhar replies "Well, I thought you knew and that was why you crossed your legs again and again when I played the ten of hearts from the table. It is called a 'criss-cross' squeeze."

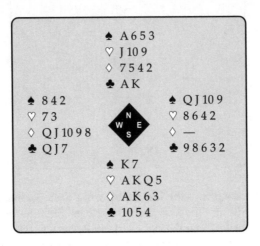

♠ A 6 5 3
♡ J 10 9
◊ 7 5 4 2
♣ A K

♠ 8 4 2
♡ 7 3
◊ Q J 10 9 8
♣ Q J 7

♠ Q J 10 9
♡ 8 6 4 2
◊ —
♣ 9 8 6 3 2

♠ K 7
♡ A K Q 5
◊ A K 6 3
♣ 10 5 4

Contract: 6♡ by South. Lead: ◊8.

"Let them, theirs is a dull life," wrote P.G. Wodehouse*. Appropriately applicable to many Bridge players the world over, both male . . . and female.

*This quotation is from *Sam the Sudden,* one of the immortal writer's several classic books. Sam had become a 'do-it-now ' practitioner ever since he saw the words on an office table. One day, Sam was taking his beloved around the courtyard of a British castle (where else?) and suddenly felt an impulse to kiss her. Do it now, said the mind. He did it then and there. "Sam, don't. The scullery-maids are watching." It was in reply to this reproach that Sam uttered the above words.

If only Pelham Grenville Wodehouse had written a book on Bridge!

Moments of Truth at the Bridge Table

INFERENTIAL BIDDING

R aju Tolani is a writer's delight. An alumnus of the prestigious Benares Hindu University, one of India's oldest such institutions, he has been a 'steel' man all his life. Currently, he is the Country Manager (India) of a giant French steel-making company. He has been a bilingual stage actor and he is a raconteur par excellence. His narration of side-splitting anecdotes are legendary in Indian Bridge circles and he has a set of tips on how to qualify for elimination in Bridge tournaments.

At the Bridge table, he is a 'different' kind of player and a master in the art of disarming his opponents. Here is an example taken from the quarter-finals of the Indian Nationals held late last year. Raju was looking at a hand with 7 high-card points and the opponents were bidding themselves to glory. On the fourth round of bidding, Raju's partner Vinay Desai came up with a lead-directional double, after which Raju came up with a classic inferential bid on the fifth round of bidding! "Occasionally, the opponents bid for you," said Raju to me.

Raju (South, hands have been rotated), vulnerable against non-vulnerable, was looking at ♠9 8 7 5 4 ♡6 ♢10 5 4 ♣A Q J 5 and the bidding proceeded thus:

West	North	East	South
	Pass	1♡	Pass
1NT¹	Pass	2♢	Pass
2♠²	Pass	3♢	Pass
3♠³	Dbl	Pass	Pass
4♢	Pass	Pass	?

¹Forcing
²Massive diamond fit, minimum
  five cards
³I would like to explore the possibility
  of game; if you have something in
  spades, bid 3NT.

Moments of Truth at the Bridge Table   117

It was Raju's turn now and most players in his position would have routinely passed – but here is what went through Raju's mind.

RHO has five hearts and four diamonds. He does not have any high cards in spades. Since LHO is marked with five diamonds, partner has only one in that suit. Partner has doubled spades and since RHO has nothing in that suit, whatever missing high cards there are in spades are with LHO. Since LHO has not supported hearts at any stage, he can at most have two cards in the suit. Which means that partner probably has six red cards, five in hearts and a singleton diamond. Partner, therefore, has seven black cards; he may even have four spades. If I can assume that the club king is on my right, in a spade contract I have one loser in hearts, one in diamonds, probably one in spades and none in clubs. I can make four spades!"

Raju bid 4♠, West doubled and the contract was made. If this is not inferential bidding, I wonder what is.

The full layout:

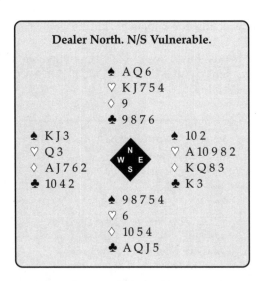

Contract: 4♠ by South, doubled. Lead: ♡Q.

Spades break 3-2, the black suit finesses are on, one diamond is ruffed on the table and the other discarded on the established jack of hearts. Raju is home.

"But a diamond lead and continuation beats the contract. In fact, even a trump lead beats the contract, but that must have been the last thing that would have been in West's mind," I said to Raju.

The gentleman that Raju is, he probably felt he must defend his opponents. "You must look from West's point of view. His partner has opened the bidding, he is himself holding eleven points with a doubleton honour in partner's suit. He is looking at a possible five hundred: give East ace and king of hearts, or ace-jack with the king in dummy, and the king of diamonds; if declarer holds two hearts, the defence can collect the first five tricks. I agree the lead was unfortunate, but it was not unreasonable."

"But that three spades call, was it not over ambitious?"

"Look, Jay, we were silent throughout. We could not muster even a simple overcall. When that happens, just a little complacency does set in. If the asked-for three no trump had indeed come over three spades, West may possibly have tried four hearts."

"With those three small clubs staring at him?"

"I asked West this question and he told me: 'The three spades call was intended to find out whether partner had a supporting honour in the suit, here the queen. Give East Q-x, A-K-J-x-x, K-Q-x-x, x-x – not an unlikely holding – and we may have a comfortable four hearts,' is what he told me. And I think that makes sense."

"It does indeed."

> "It is possible to see without being seen," the army man will tell you. On the Bridge table, it is *not* possible to bid without being understood . . . by the opponents!

DISCOVERING
THE UNEXPECTED

by
Professor Mayank Dholakiya

Professor Mayank Dholakiya is one of India's leading management thinkers. An alumnus of the Indian Institute of Management, Ahmedabad, and the President's gold medal winner from the Institute of Cost and Works Accountants of India, he is currently Dean of the Faculty of Management Studies, Maharaja Sayajirao University, Baroda, India. His e-mail address is: mayankd@yahoo.com

An extended meaning of truth

Life is a fascinating journey. Every step along the way presents us with opportunities and challenges. There are countless times when we can exercise our option to act, and turn specific moments into moments of magic. This happens when we seize that chance, bite the bullet and stretch out a little more to make things happen.

We need to understand more about the truth of the events that we experience in life. Experts have postulated that truth is a dynamic relation between an idea and an existing reality. Truth, therefore, is not a static phenomenon embedded in an idea or a possibility of a particular action. Truth, thus, creates possible consequences for action. At a given specific point of time, the integrity of the moment itself can suddenly reveal how to respond to events. As Henri Bergson argues in his classic book *The Creative Mind: An Introduction to Metaphysics*, truth is not a static relation of correspondence to an unchanging, predetermined state of being. Truth is an active relation between an idea and events that may change according to the flow of reality.

What are moments of truth?

Moments of truth can be seen as critical decision-points we reach in life, when we make unexpected discoveries, particularly when we were not looking for them. It may be when 'dreams come true,' (we may have been 'dreaming' for years) or when 'prayers are answered,' (we may have been praying for years). Or it may happen that we wake up one morning suddenly to realise that what we did in a particular situation the day before was not appropriate.

But are moments of truth mere chance discoveries? Is there no role for our knowledge, experience or insight for deciding that moment? Let us explore.

Moments of truth and serendipity

What happens or what we do at these moments of truth can be likened to serendipity. Serendipity, a word coined by Horace Walpole, is the faculty of making happy and chance discoveries by accident, of things one is not in quest of. It refers to a unique mix of accident and wisdom or sagacity, in being able to identify the significance of a discovery. The phrase was derived from the story of three young princes of Serendip (now known as Sri Lanka), who, on their journeys around the world, came across such discoveries. In the realm of qualitative research, a lot of work has been done to probe the concept of serendipity and how this concept finds applications in various processes by which we use the temporal (over a time line), relational and analytical aspects of serendipity. Researchers have tended to conclude that serendipity is not a matter of pure chance, but an "interactive outcome" of a unique combination of insight and intuition, coupled with chance.

Moments of truth and scientific discoveries

A lot of scientific discoveries can also be seen as moments of truth. Whether it is Archimedes shouting "Eureka!" having discovered the law of hydrostatics, or Isaac Newton having an apple falling on his head to discover the law of gravity, or Bequerel discovering radioactivity by accidentally throwing uranium salts into a drawer containing photographic materials, all these were not merely surprise occurrences. Thomas Kuhn, in his fascinating *Structure of Scientific Revolutions*, argues that scientific breakthroughs largely depended on a critical yet unexpected insight that led to a 'better' way of understanding empirical relations as a new paradigm. We may state that while scientific pursuits may be a chaotic or chancy process, an approximation to truth is possible, which occurs in a flash at a given moment. Moments of truth can help us suddenly develop a deeper understanding of a given situation or a state of being that we may already be aware of.

Moments of truth are not mere happenstances

There is a vital point to be understood here. A moment of truth is not mere happenstance. It is not merely a chance occurrence that we just want to make sense of. The key lies in appreciating our mistakes and learning from them. As we stumble upon events, each event can become the basis of subsequent insight. The flow of events in a Bridge game can help us set up a process of reformulating our strategies, or building new ways of looking at options. And when the moment of truth arrives, everything falls into place like a unique kaleidoscope pattern and an unexpected outcome follows.

Moments of truth and inductive research

Moments of truth can also be seen through the laws of inductive research. This relates to the analytical dimension of serendipity. This dimension involves the ability of researchers to relate data to theory which leads to relevant insights. The deductive research approach implies that we know what we are looking for before we find it. On the other hand, inductive research models actually position insight into the chosen stance of analysis, making it plausible to reach several conclusions from the same data. How does a Bridge player prise the moment of truth to his advantage through the inductive reasoning process? How does this flash of insight occur? First of all, as we observe or capture data, we feed them into our mental grid based on our earlier experiences and knowledge. We, thus, create a template for new understanding. Suddenly, one sees the linkages, cause and effect relationships, and the fresh view of the relevance of the situation, as was not noticed before. In our effort of sense-making at the table, available data either talk to the player, or play off each other. This all produces what marketers of today's products and services call the 'ah-ha' effect. This leads on to the next stage. The player may discover a unique strategic response, as analytical serendipity helps one to look at the problem with a fresh perspective. We can make, and see beyond, powerful and unexpected connections. The entire process evolves into a surprise action which can turn the moment of truth into a moment of magic!

Moments of truth are allies!

Sometimes, the unplanned or unpredicted occurrences are our own creation. It is the way we have been mentally scripted and the way we have learnt to work in a situation that makes us commit mistakes. The significant point is: can we make sense out of our errors? Yes, errors of insight can be converted into insight out of errors!

Acting in the moment of truth involves, therefore, examining the unexamined fusion of possibilities that brings about appreciation of chance events as relevant and meaningful. We deploy, as a consequence, fresh insights from a mosaic of relations and then connect to surprise events.

And then, we win the moment of truth.

PREVAILING OVER
TOP DEFENCE

Ajay Khare is one of the quietest of the top dozen or so Indian players and he gives one the impression of being a deep thinker as well. He was one of the finalists in the World Open Pairs at Albuquerque in 1994, and the manner in which he sent me details of a few deals over e-mail makes me believe that he must be very methodical in his approach to the game.

Here is Ajay in action, as declarer, South, in an Indian National Pairs event in April this year.

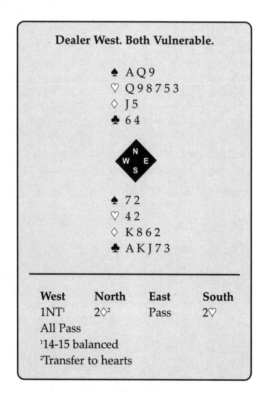

Dealer West. Both Vulnerable.

```
              ♠ A Q 9
              ♡ Q 9 8 7 5 3
              ◊ J 5
              ♣ 6 4
                     N
                  W     E
                     S
              ♠ 7 2
              ♡ 4 2
              ◊ K 8 6 2
              ♣ A K J 7 3
```

West	North	East	South
1NT[1]	2◊[2]	Pass	2♡
All Pass			

[1]14-15 balanced
[2]Transfer to hearts

Contract: 2♡ by South. Lead: ♡J.

On Ajay's left was a member of an Indian team that reached the last sixteen for the Power Rosenblum trophy during the World Championships in Montreal last year. On his right was an Indian Master with a very good track record.

The ♡J was a deadly lead, depriving declarer of a third-round spade ruff. The lead was covered by dummy's queen and East won with the king and continued trumps, two more rounds of which were drawn by the defenders. On the third heart, East let go of a diamond and South, a club.

West now switched to the eight of spades, and Ajay called for the queen from the table which held. Ajay had only seven top tricks and there did not seem to be any hope for the eighth as West surely held the ace of diamonds – he was the no-trump opener. There was just a flicker of hope in the club suit: the queen could come down in two rounds or it could be finessed.

"My decision can wait," thought Ajay to himself and played two rounds of trumps. East discarded two clubs, Ajay disposed of two small diamonds, and West let go a spade and a diamond. It was now clear that the club finesse would not work and that West was holding that card guarded. To explore further the distribution patterns, Ajay now cashed two top clubs. East showed up with the ten, but discarded a diamond on the second club trick, West obviously following to both. Ajay now ruffed a club clearing the suit and on this trick East discarded a spade. This was the position:

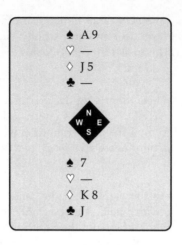

♠ A 9
♡ —
◊ J 5
♣ —

♠ 7
♡ —
◊ K 8
♣ J

Six tricks to declarer in his 2♡ contract,
three tricks to the defence. Dummy to play.

West surely had the spade king and the diamond ace. He had shown up with three hearts and three clubs. He discarded one diamond and one spade apart from the spade he played at trick four. He would not have blanked his diamond ace, so he must have had one more card in the suit. He, therefore, had two diamonds and two spades. That meant that East also had two spades and two diamonds. LHO had so far shown up with the king of spades, the ace and jack of hearts, and the queen of clubs; together with the ace of diamonds, that would come to exactly 14 points. West could not have the diamond queen because that would take him outside his no-trump range, so it had to be East who had that card.

By now Ajay had the defenders fair and square. He played the ace of spades, and West unblocked his king to no avail. The last spade had to be won by East, West following. Poor East had to open the diamonds, and it was not even a guess, it was a certainty which card had to be played. Ajay's king of diamonds was the fulfilling trick.

Neat, wasn't it? The full deal:

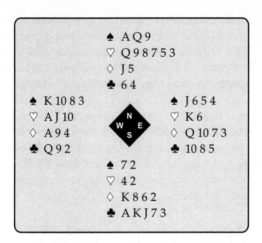

	♠ A Q 9	
	♡ Q 9 8 7 5 3	
	◊ J 5	
	♣ 6 4	
♠ K 10 8 3		♠ J 6 5 4
♡ A J 10		♡ K 6
◊ A 9 4		◊ Q 10 7 3
♣ Q 9 2		♣ 10 8 5
	♠ 7 2	
	♡ 4 2	
	◊ K 8 6 2	
	♣ A K J 7 3	

Contract: 2♡ by South. Lead: ♡J.

R. Sreedharan, Ajay's partner and dummy in this case, is also one of India's top players, and has represented the country in international events. Sreedharan is a great believer in continuously improving partnership understanding and, much later, the two got into a discussion on the above deal.

"Ajay, about the last four-card position. By that time you had correctly deduced that both opponents were holding two diamonds and two spades each. You were also sure that the diamond queen was on your right, and the ace on your left. Much earlier in the game, if West had quietly discarded two diamonds and come down to the bare ace (which you may or may not know), how would you have handled the end-position?"

"You see, I had been carefully watching the diamond discards. By the time I reached the four-card position with dummy to play, I had counted five diamond discards – two from the right, two from me and one from the left. Add the four which dummy and I were holding in the end position, the defenders must have the outstanding four. If, as you say, West had discarded one more diamond earlier on, they would have been left with only three, obviously 2-1, in which case I would have played a low diamond off the table before cashing the ace of spades. Also, East's card on the low diamond would tell me who was holding the singleton honour. I was safe either way."

"What if both defenders had cooperated with each other fully and come down thus: RHO, with three diamonds to the queen and the bare spade jack; LHO, with the bare ace of diamonds and three spades to the king? In that case, too, you would have to play a low diamond from the table, although the same four diamonds are outstanding."

"Yes, but there was another pointer earlier on. The bidding had died down early at the two level. RHO had shown up with five or six points and with his partner's opening no-trump, he would have competed with two spades if he had five. LHO cannot have five spades, because he opened a no-trump. No, they could not have misled me with their discards. I knew the spades were 4-4."

Ajay's declarer play was top class, backed by impeccable logic. Just look at the way he cashed those trump tricks early. Just see how much in advance he had deduced that the spades were 4-4. Just note how he avoided the club finesse – the uninitiated might argue that finessing in clubs, with the spade ace intact, is another way of making the contract, not realising that that play would require a 3-3 break in clubs.

There is one more thing worthy of mention here. East sort of over-played his discards early on. On the third heart, East threw a diamond. On the fourth and fifth hearts East threw two clubs. With the spade ace still in dummy and only four clubs outstanding at that stage, Ajay could have asked for a low club from the table and covered whatever card East played to ensure that three club tricks were available. In fact, if the declarer were able to duck a small club to West early on, he would succeed if clubs broke 3-3 or the queen doubleton came down.

> The best in you is often brought out by the best against you.

A RARE SUIT COMBINATION

Chennai-based technocrat, P. Sridhar, represented India in the Bridge Federation of Asia and the Middle East (BFAME) tournament at Colombo three years ago and in the Bridge Championships preceding the Commonwealth Games in Manchester last year. He has also won numerous Indian titles, including the Indian Nationals in 2001. When I received the details of the following deal which he had played, my first thought was to look up "Suit Combinations" in *The Bridge Players' Encyclopedia*, 1967 edition, edited by Ben Cohen and Rhoda Barrow and published by Paul Hamlyn Ltd, London. The section dealt with how declarer should play specific suit combinations in order to get a specified number of tricks. I was able to narrow down to VB(c) where:

'V' referred to cases where the defence had four points
'B' referred to cases where the missing honour cards are king and jack
'(c)' referred to cases where declarer and dummy together held seven cards

There were twenty-four suit combinations listed under the above heading, but unfortunately for me, I could not find the suit combinations which Sridhar encountered and played in a pairs event. He was looking at Q-10-8-4 opposite dummy's A-6-5 and he had to play for three tricks in the suit. Fortunately for him there were other indications available to him; unfortunately for him, there were limitations also.

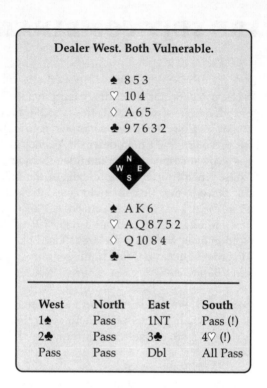

Dealer West. Both Vulnerable.

```
        ♠ 8 5 3
        ♡ 10 4
        ◇ A 6 5
        ♣ 9 7 6 3 2

              N
          W       E
              S

        ♠ A K 6
        ♡ A Q 8 7 5 2
        ◇ Q 10 8 4
        ♣ —
```

West	North	East	South
1♠	Pass	1NT	Pass (!)
2♣	Pass	3♣	4♡ (!)
Pass	Pass	Dbl	All Pass

Contract: 4♡ by South. Lead: ♣K.

The bidding needs some explanation. The deal occurred in the finals of
a pairs event and Sridhar had calculated that if a top could be obtained,
he could be in contention for the winner's prize. The 1♠ on his left
promised five cards, the 1NT was non-forcing, the pass was the first
step in the strategy, the 2♣ bid showed at least four cards and 3♣
should be construed as a normal four-card immediate raise. Sridhar
now realised that the bidding could die at this level and 'gambled'
with a bid of 4♡, promptly doubled by East.

The lead of king of clubs denied the ace. Let us take it from there.

Sridhar could count nine of West's cards, five spades and four clubs.
Give him queen-jack of spades, king-queen-maybe-jack of clubs, he
needs to hold at least at least one red king – if not both – for his
opening bid. If it is both, RHO has only the club ace and possible a jack
or two to make that 1NT response, and then double the contract as

Moments of Truth at the Bridge Table

well. No, it is not possible: RHO must have one of the red kings. If it is the heart king, it can be finessed, but there will still be a heart loser. The ace of diamonds is the only entry to the table and you need to play diamonds also from the table. You cannot finesse in hearts *and* play a diamond from the table. There is a definite heart loser, the spade loser also cannot go anywhere, and there is at least one diamond loser. If this contract has to be made, it is vital to restrict the diamond losers to one. How about a singleton king of diamonds in the West hand? The he will be holding three hearts (nine black cards are known) and the heart king will be on the right, doubleton. No that will not do either, because you can play a diamond from the table *or* finesse the hearts, and you require both.

What about a singleton heart king with West? That also will not help you: you have a definite heart loser, may even be two to RHO. Resigned to at least one loser in each of the three suits, Sridhar cashed the ace of hearts after ruffing the club lead. Nothing sensational happened, West contributed the six and East the three. He continued with a low heart (is there any other play?), and happily the king appeared from the left. So far, so good but there were still miles to go. West continued clubs and Sridhar had to ruff again. He drew the last trump from East and paused for thought.

Nine black cards and two in hearts would mean West had only two diamonds. Should Sridhar play a low diamond from both hands hoping for another king doubleton in the West hand? The second round ace could draw the king, and the jack on the right could be finessed immediately thereafter. Good thought this, but Sridhar himself had concluded earlier that one red king was with East! It was illogical to go back on that now and it was more or less certain that RHO held four diamonds along with the king. How about the jack, where was it, could it be favourably located?

There seemed to be . . . there definitely was one chance, and that was for West to hold the jack of diamonds and another card, whatever that card was! So run the queen of diamonds on the first round losing to the king on the right. The ace now draws the jack and if the nine has not appeared earlier from the left, a small diamond off the table is led to the ten-eight in hand! *Oh, la, la!*

The full hand:

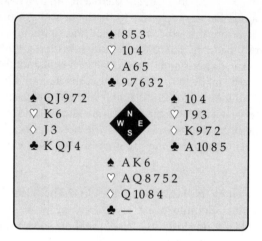

```
              ♠ 8 5 3
              ♡ 10 4
              ◇ A 6 5
              ♣ 9 7 6 3 2
♠ Q J 9 7 2                    ♠ 10 4
♡ K 6           N              ♡ J 9 3
◇ J 3        W     E           ◇ K 9 7 2
♣ K Q J 4       S              ♣ A 10 8 5
              ♠ A K 6
              ♡ A Q 8 7 5 2
              ◇ Q 10 8 4
              ♣ —
```

Enormous work has been done in the field of suit combinations and very accurate guidelines have been drawn on how to play these combinations for either the maximum tricks possible, or one fewer trick, two fewer tricks, etc. In some situations, however, the optimum method of playing the suit in isolation may not be enough. The play of one suit may be conditioned by other factors, like the totality of the hand and the availability of entries (as in the above case). When one encounters such situations on the table, more often than not, the solution also may present itself. This is precisely what Professor Mayank Dholakiya has suggested when he says: 'available data either talk to the player or play off each other.' (See page 122.)

There is no substitute for experiencing a problem at the table *and* solving it there!

THE PIP-WATCHING PARTNER

Partners are a rare breed and a class by themselves. In my earlier book on Bridge, I had this to say: "By definition, partnership guarantees equality of relationship. There is no such thing, there can be such thing, as a senior partner, at least in Bridge.It is like saying 'free gift.' A gift is a gift, always free. Who has paid for a gift?"

Still, most Bridge partners behave as if they were the 'senior' ones. In this class of 'senior ones,' there is a special sub-section called the 'omniscientists'. They are the regular after-the-event experts and almost all of them are insufferable when they have been dummy in a deal where you were the declarer. A case in point is the following:

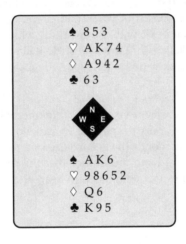

This was a simple 1♡ – 4♡ auction without any intervention by the opponents.

West leads the four of spades, third or fifth best. Your RHO puts in the queen and you win with the ace. You play a low heart, ten from the left, ace from the table and the three from the right. You ask for a low diamond from the table, East goes up with the king and continues with the two of spades which you win with the king. You can discard your losing spade on the ace of diamonds, but you need miracles to make this contract. You cash the diamond queen on which West plays the ten. You play a second heart to dummy's top card, but RHO shows out. So, you have a heart loser as well!

But you are a never-say-die declarer. You cash the ace of diamonds discarding your losing spade and down comes the jack from your left. The nine of diamonds is good now, but is it good enough for your contract? What about your two remaining clubs?

If you cash the nine of diamonds now, discarding a club from hand, LHO will ruff and play a spade which you will have to ruff in hand. You have been careful enough in your heart play; you can still enter the table in the suit and then lead a club from dummy hoping that the club ace is with your RHO.

LHO's lead was third or fifth best. It is now clear that it was third best. You have already disposed of your spade loser. If you ruff dummy's third spade now, and exit with a third heart which LHO has to win, what would he be left with? Only clubs! He will be forced to open the suit giving your king a trick, and your third club can be ruffed in dummy!

Congratulating yourself on your good thinking, you ask for a small spade from the table and your partner winces; you see, he had almost tabled the nine of diamonds (he is not supposed to do that, of course). You ruff the spade in hand and notice that the jack has come down from the left. You now exit with the third heart and West is end-played.

The full deal:

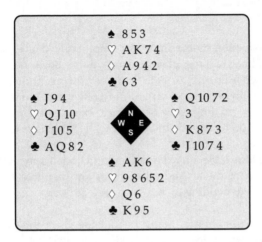

```
              ♠ 8 5 3
              ♡ A K 7 4
              ◇ A 9 4 2
              ♣ 6 3
  ♠ J 9 4                    ♠ Q 10 7 2
  ♡ Q J 10          N        ♡ 3
  ◇ J 10 5      W      E     ◇ K 8 7 3
  ♣ A Q 8 2         S        ♣ J 10 7 4
              ♠ A K 6
              ♡ 9 8 6 5 2
              ◇ Q 6
              ♣ K 9 5
```

Your partner in this case is about fifteen years senior to you in age and about twenty years senior to you in terms of Bridge. He observes wryly in front of your opponents "That nine of diamonds was good, man!"

You can do no better than agree with the 'senior.'

THIS DEUCE IS DIFFERENT!

Wimbledon centre court. The umpire calls deuce, whether it is John McEnroe playing Bjorn Borg, Boris Becker playing Stefan Edberg, or Pete Sampras playing André Agassi. You may call the atmosphere electric or any other such adjective. To my mind, there is no English word which can do full justice to that atmosphere. You have to be there and feel it. Nothing else will do.

But at the Bridge table, there is another kind of deuce available. In fact, there are four of them. And all of them are harmless little ones or deadly devils, depending on how you look at them.

A heated discussion was going on outside the venue of a Bridge tournament where a Swiss Teams round had just ended. Most of the players, a few of them agitated, had score-sheets in their hands. One group of four was really wrought-up and I was standing a few feet away. They wanted me to arbitrate. In one room, this particular team's opponents had bid and made 4♠. In the other room, the pair of this team had stopped in 2♠ and, to add salt to the wound, had gone one down in the contract. "How can such a thing happen?", asked one of the players against whom 4♠ was bid and made.

"Obviously it happened, no? Tell me how," I said.

This was the deal:

```
                  Dealer South.
                  N/S Vulnerable.

                  ♠ 9 8 6 2
                  ♡ A 8 4
                  ◇ Q 10 3
                  ♣ K 7 6

                        N
                   W         E
                        S

                  ♠ A K 10 7 3
                  ♡ 5
                  ◇ K J 6 4
                  ♣ J 8 5
```

In both rooms, West overcalled in clubs after South had opened 1♠ and in one room North bid an ultra-conservative 2♠ and there the auction ended. The other room North was the adventurous type: he bid game in spades straightaway after the club overcall.

In both rooms, the lead was the two of diamonds. At the table where the contract was 4♠, East won the opening lead with the ace and continued the suit which West ruffed. West tried a low club now, but there was no way for declarer to go wrong. He went up with the king and ultimately lost only one ruff, the diamond ace and the club ace. Four bid, four made.

At the other table where 2♠ was the final contract, East won the diamond lead with the ace and played back the two of clubs; West won with the ace, and continued the suit. Sure that the club suit was going to be ruffed on his right, declarer asked for a low club from the table. East won with the queen and played back a diamond which West ruffed. Now, a club from West was ruffed by East who played back another diamond for West to ruff. The first six tricks went to the defence, one in diamonds, two in clubs and the three ruffs. One down!

The full deal:

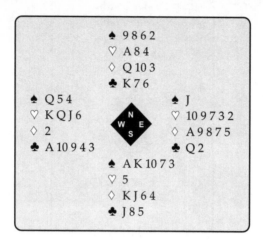

```
                    ♠ 9 8 6 2
                    ♡ A 8 4
                    ◇ Q 10 3
                    ♣ K 7 6
  ♠ Q 5 4                          ♠ J
  ♡ K Q J 6         N              ♡ 10 9 7 3 2
  ◇ 2            W     E           ◇ A 9 8 7 5
  ♣ A 10 9 4 3      S              ♣ Q 2
                    ♠ A K 10 7 3
                    ♡ 5
                    ◇ K J 6 4
                    ♣ J 8 5
```

To divert the group's attention, I asked: "Is four hearts making for East-West?"

"With the club suit good for four tricks, four hearts should be cold on any lead," replied the brightest of the lot. He then asked me: "But tell us, sir, should not declarer go up with the club king when West continues the suit?"

"You are right in a way. The deuce from the left is definitely a singleton, because it was led. The deuce from the right may or may not be a singleton. If both the deuces are singletons and the trumps are 2-2, the defence will wrap up the first six tricks. However, if trumps are 3-1, there is only one diamond ruff available to the defence and it does not matter if you lose three club tricks. This means that declarer can afford to play the club king in case the deuce from the right is not a singleton. "

> Deuces tell stories. Different deuces tell different stories.

AN ARISTOCRATIC DEFENCE

B ridge is a game of aristocrats.

Two Indian names come readily to mind: the first is Jagdish Kohli, who was a member of the R.R. Ruia's team (RR was one of the founding vice-presidents of the World Bridge Federation) that was the first Indian team to participate in a world championships in the early sixties. Kohli has a mention in *The Bridge Players' Encyclopedia*.

The other is 'Sam' Quadri.

I.M. Quadri, nicknamed 'Sam', is one of the quietest, coolest and nicest Bridge players India has ever produced. Along with his illustrious partner B.M. Malani, Sam has been a consistent winner of several Indian tournaments during the seventies. Malani and Sam were the perfect foil for each other. While the former used to produce almost impossible card-plays, rumbustiously so to speak, the latter was soundness personified.

The following deal is about an 'aristocratic' defence brought about by a twenty-three-year-old engineer against Sam. The deal occurred in a local tournament at Hyderabad in South India in the year 1979.

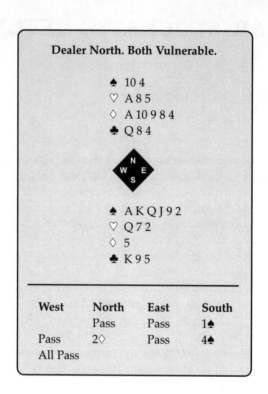

♠ 10 4
♡ A 8 5
♢ A 10 9 8 4
♣ Q 8 4

♠ A K Q J 9 2
♡ Q 7 2
♢ 5
♣ K 9 5

West	North	East	South
	Pass	Pass	1♠
Pass	2♢	Pass	4♠
All Pass			

Contract: 4♠ by South. Lead: ♢2.

Sitting South as declarer was Sam Quadri. He won the opening lead with dummy's ace, and then ruffed the four of diamonds with the ace of trumps, as the king of diamonds came down from his left. There is no knowing what went through Sam's mind at that stage but he surely must have wondered: "The leads these IIT-ians (Indian Institute of Technology) make these days!" Sitting West was R. Krishnan, all of twenty-three years old, who had earned the nickname 'Kista' from his college mates.

At trick three, Sam cashed his king of spades and then played a low spade to dummy's ten, noting that both opponents followed suit. The eight of diamonds from the table fetched a low diamond from the right and Sam discarded the five of clubs. Kista ruffed with the eight of spades.

A ruff to the defence on this trump layout? Yes, indeed.

Out comes the ten of clubs from the West hand and Sam wins in hand with the king to arrive at:

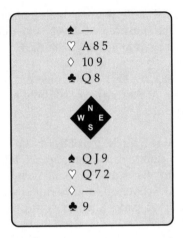

```
        ♠ —
        ♡ A 8 5
        ◊ 10 9
        ♣ Q 8

             N
          W     E
             S

        ♠ Q J 9
        ♡ Q 7 2
        ◊ —
        ♣ 9
```

Sam now lets the club nine run and East produces the jack and switches to the ten of hearts. Down one. The full deal:

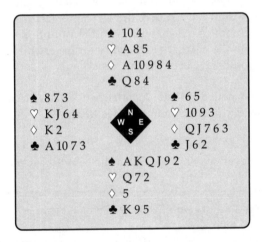

```
                ♠ 10 4
                ♡ A 8 5
                ◊ A 10 9 8 4
                ♣ Q 8 4
    ♠ 8 7 3                   ♠ 6 5
    ♡ K J 6 4                 ♡ 10 9 3
    ◊ K 2        N            ◊ Q J 7 6 3
    ♣ A 10 7 3  W   E         ♣ J 6 2
                 S
                ♠ A K Q J 9 2
                ♡ Q 7 2
                ◊ 5
                ♣ K 9 5
```

There are quite a few points of interest in the deal.

- As the cards lie, one way of making the contract would have been to draw three rounds of trumps, a club to dummy's queen, and a high diamond from the table discarding a low heart from hand, to end-play West. *But* – tell me what declarer would assume the lead of a deuce from a holding of king-deuce?

- Sam did try for a fairly reasonable line of play: a 4-3 break in diamonds and the club ace with West. Note that Sam still had the last resort of the heart king being with East.

- That smooth duck by East on the nine of clubs takes guts and Bridge character. At that stage, West's only hope was for declarer to misguess in clubs.

- If East is allowed to hold the ten of hearts, he must either continue hearts or play a club to defeat the contract. If he carelessly tries a diamond honour, the squeeze count rectification would have taken place and declarer could have ruffed the diamond in hand and run the last two spades to inflict a heart-club squeeze on West.

- A heart at any stage by West gives away the contract. Which is precisely what happened at the other table where a heart was led.

- East also played his part. If he had covered the eight of diamonds, declarer would have ruffed, drawn West's last trump, played a club to dummy's queen, and taken the ruffing diamond finesse again, with the heart ace as an entry for the established diamond which would have been the tenth trick!

Deal over, Sam smiled at Kista. To the twenty-three year old, that smile must have been worth a hundred Bridge trophies.

Twenty-four years hence – from 1979 to 2003 – Kista is today one of India's top players having played for the country several times over.

> Bridge is a mind game. To succeed, you have to be one step ahead . . . mentally.

EIGHT SPOTS ARE WORTH 210 POINTS

Arun Bapat is a chemical engineer from Benares Hindu University, who has been an ardent Bridge player for several years now. I saw him employ a simple defensive stratagem during the preliminary stages of the Indian Team Selection Trials held in Bombay in May 2003.

With both sides vulnerable, you are Arun, sitting West and looking at ♠ A K 3 ♡ K J 9 4 ◊ Q 9 8 ♣ A 10 3. Dealer South, playing a strong no-trump and five-card majors, opens 1◊ and you overcall with 1NT, 15-17 – maybe a poor 18. North passes and East comes in with 2♠, passed around to North who competes with three diamonds which is passed round to you. You consider bidding 3♠, but ultimately you pass, deciding that +100 is more likely than +140.

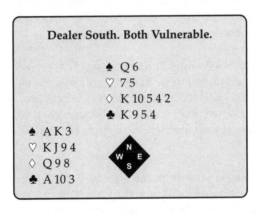

Dealer South. Both Vulnerable.

```
               ♠ Q 6
               ♡ 7 5
               ◊ K 10 5 4 2
               ♣ K 9 5 4
    ♠ A K 3              N
    ♡ K J 9 4         W     E
    ◊ Q 9 8              S
    ♣ A 10 3
```

Contract: 3 ◊ by South. Lead: ♠A.

You cash the two spade honours and realise that you are now faced with Hobson's choice. A spade continuation now would probably provide declarer with a ruff-and-discard and any other card would give away a possible trick. You console yourself by thinking that declarer is anyway likely to finesse in diamonds through you, so you might as well play a diamond. Declarer wins with the jack in hand, partner following. Declarer now draws two more rounds of trumps, ending in hand, partner discarding two small spades. Declarer now plays the two of clubs in this position:

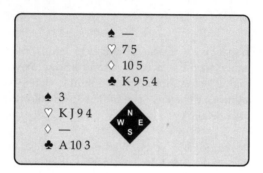

Can you see it coming? It is your turn now ; which is the card you are going to play and why? By this stage you know that declarer started off with two spades and four diamonds. That gives him seven cards between hearts and clubs. He does not have five hearts, since he did not open 1♡ He does not have five clubs either, because that would mean that partner held 6-5 in the majors in which case he would have competed further.

Declarer is either 4-3 or 3-4 in hearts-clubs. What about his high-card strength? He has turned up with five points in diamonds and none in spades. What is left is the ace and queen in hearts, and the queen and jack in clubs. He may have all the four honours, but that would mean partner competed with the mere spade jack. No, partner has a point or two more.

The worst scenario is when partner holds the club jack in addition to his spade jack. You will still win two club tricks all right even if the declarer has the club queen (which he probably has), and it is important that partner wins one of the club tricks to enable him to make that all important switch to hearts. Otherwise, you will be end-played. If you casually play the three of clubs, declarer will win with the king on the table, ask for a second club from the table and play the queen only when East plays the jack – and you will be end-played.

Is there a way out? Yes, if partner holds three clubs which include the eight in addition to his jack, you can succeed by playing the ten. This

Moments of Truth at the Bridge Table

will cost a club trick if partner started with doubleton jack, but if you play low instead of the ten, you will lose your heart trick as you will be end-played on the third round of clubs.

Arun Bapat saw the end play coming, hoped partner had three clubs including the jack and the eight, played the ten on the first round of the suit and ensured, the defeat of the contract. Minus 110 has been converted to plus 100, a gain of 210 points!

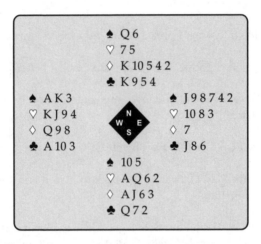

It is not enough to be merely 'aware' of what is happening around us. We need to be truly 'tuned in'.

THE WHY-BECAUSE AXIOM

'Plan your play,' is an age-old Bridge maxim. It often happens, however, that there are alternative plans of play available and the astute Bridge player chooses a particular plan of play on the basis that if Plan A fails, he has recourse to Plan B, and if that also fails, he can resort to Plan C.

It all boils down to what I prefer to call 'the why-because axiom'.

"Why Plan A first? To me, Plan C appears to be a better proposition."

"Because Plan A does not endanger my contract, and I can try Plan B and Plan C later."

"Why not try Plan C before Plan B at least?"

"Because if I try Plan C, I cannot go back to Plan B and I will have to abandon it altogether."

See what I mean? The hallmark of a good Bridge player is the ability to continuously ask himself 'why' and to come out with a logically convincing 'because'. Here is an example:

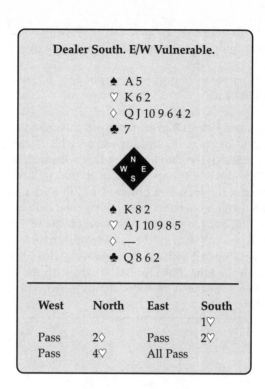

Dealer South. E/W Vulnerable.

♠ A 5
♡ K 6 2
♢ Q J 10 9 6 4 2
♣ 7

♠ K 8 2
♡ A J 10 9 8 5
♢ —
♣ Q 8 6 2

West	North	East	South
			1♡
Pass	2♢	Pass	2♡
Pass	4♡	All Pass	

Contract: 4♡ by South. Lead: ♠J.

A very fundamental question first. Where do you win the first trick and why? The answers to these questions can be given only after you have formulated a plan of play.

You have to take care of your-black suit losers. A couple of them could be ruffed on the table, but a couple may not be enough because you may misguess the trump suit and lose a trick to the queen. How about split honours in the diamond suit? You do not seem to have enough entries to the table to enjoy the established diamond suit after drawing trumps. How about trying for three ruffs on the table? Even if the opponents play a heart, it will give you a free finesse, won't it? Think again: a free finesse is of no use to you, because the defender with the queen may not play the queen and dummy's king of trumps is needed for a ruff. How about a trump reduction in hand so as to make all six of South's trumps? There is something in that, but it may fail if West started off with queen-small or better in hearts, in which case the trump coup will not work. The most frustrating aspect of this deal is that you know nothing of the defenders' hand patterns.

You decide to try for three ruffs on the table, and if it fails, hope for six trump tricks in hand.

You win the spade jack lead on the table, ruff a diamond small, cash the king of spades, and play the third spade on which West puts up the ten; dummy discards the club loser, but East wins with the queen and switches to the three of trumps. You put in the eight which holds as West contributes the four. You now ruff a club with dummy's small trump, ruff a diamond in hand, and ruff a second club with the table's trump king. You ask for the third diamond off the table; East puts in the ace which you ruff with your ten, and West's diamond king comes crashing down. You exit with a small club; West wins with the jack and continues with the king, but East has to win with the ace. East now plays the seven of hearts in the following two-card ending:

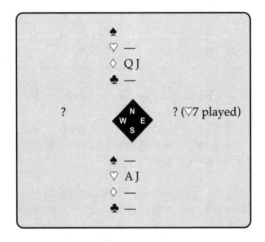

Declarer has to make both tricks for his contract.

They have defended skillfully. You now know that diamonds were 3-3 and clubs 4-4. The clincher is the spade suit. Is it 5-3 giving East three hearts, *or* is it 4-4 for the hearts to break 2-2? The nine and seven of spades are missing ; is East holding one of them, probably the nine?

Remember your Plan B? You had hoped to make all six of South's trumps. But you had also concluded that the trump coup may not work as West might hold queen-small or better in hearts. Go back to the third spade won by East. Both defenders are excellent players, and you have no doubt that this West would have been quite capable of pushing through a heart if he had won the third spade. East probably won the third spade because he had to. He does not seem to hold any more spades which means he has the heart queen. You decide to play the jack and you are home! The full deal:

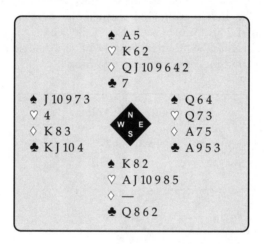

```
                    ♠ A 5
                    ♡ K 6 2
                    ◇ Q J 10 9 6 4 2
                    ♣ 7
   ♠ J 10 9 7 3              ♠ Q 6 4
   ♡ 4            N          ♡ Q 7 3
   ◇ K 8 3      W   E        ◇ A 7 5
   ♣ K J 10 4     S          ♣ A 9 5 3
                    ♠ K 8 2
                    ♡ A J 10 9 8 5
                    ◇ —
                    ♣ Q 8 6 2
```

There is one other pointer.

It is a rare occurrence, statistically speaking, for two partners to have the same hand pattern. If declarer had played for the drop of the trump queen, he would have been effectively playing for both defenders to hold the same number of cards in each of the four suits, 4-2-3-4, which is very rare indeed!

End-plays produce exhilarating end results.

MORE OFTEN THAN NOT, SOMETHING DEVELOPS

The following deal has been taken from the finals of the Indian Team Selection Trials played in Bombay in May 2003. Sitting South was K.R. Venkataraman (Venky to friends) who was a member of the Indian team that reached the quarter-finals of the Bermuda Bowl 2001. Venky was also in the team that reached the Round of Sixteen at the Montreal World Championships, 2002. Hands have been rotated for convenience of reporting.

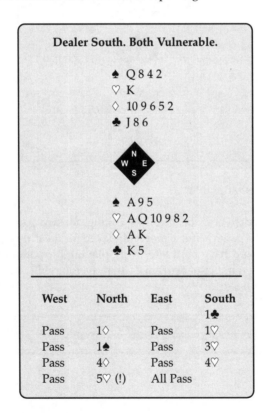

Dealer South. Both Vulnerable.

```
                 ♠ Q 8 4 2
                 ♡ K
                 ◊ 10 9 6 5 2
                 ♣ J 8 6

                      N
                  W       E
                      S

                 ♠ A 9 5
                 ♡ A Q 10 9 8 2
                 ◊ A K
                 ♣ K 5
```

West	North	East	South
			1♣
Pass	1◊	Pass	1♡
Pass	1♠	Pass	3♡
Pass	4◊	Pass	4♡
Pass	5♡ (!)	All Pass	

Contract: 5♡ by South. Lead: ♡3.

Venky opened a strong 1♣ and eventually found himself in a stretched (shall we say 'failed-slam-try') contract of 5♡. He won the trump lead on the table, crossed to a diamond honour and drew two more rounds of trumps, relieved that they broke 3-3. So far, so good. But this contract seemed to be doomed. Why, even 4♡ cannot make if both black suits behave badly. After drawing trumps, Venky cashed his other diamond honour on which East played the queen. What were Venky's chances?

To get to eleven tricks, Venky needed the club king to make and also the spade queen to make, unless the diamonds broke 3-3 and the opponents could be forced to play a third diamond with the spade queen as a possible entry for the established diamonds. A little far-fetched, of course.

The kibitzer spirit in us would prompt us to comment that Venky should have tried a club on winning with the heart king on the table, placing the ace with East. But a player of Venky's class would reply that the spade queen making is an essential condition, a *sine qua non*, for the contract to succeed. If it is so, the club play could very well come later.

At the table, Venky's never-say-die spirit probably hoped that a chance might present itself. He first considered a 3-3 break in spades with the king on the left. But he decided against that because West was Rajesh Dalal, his team-mate both in Paris and Montreal, who was well capable of winning the spade king only on the third round of the suit effectively to scuttle dummy's thirteenth spade.

At trick six, Venky cashed the ace of spades, perhaps to see what might develop (or was it for want of something better to do?), on which the ten appeared from the left, and then he played the nine of spades in this position:

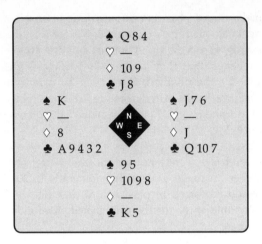

```
                    ♠ Q 8 4
                    ♡ —
                    ◇ 10 9
                    ♣ J 8
    ♠ K                           ♠ J 7 6
    ♡ —           N               ♡ —
    ◇ 8        W     E            ◇ J
    ♣ A 9 4 3 2      S            ♣ Q 10 7
                    ♠ 9 5
                    ♡ 10 9 8
                    ◇ —
                    ♣ K 5
```

Six tricks to declarer in his 5♡ contract.
None to the defence. Declarer plays ♠9.

On winning with the spade king, Rajesh had no safe exit. If he played a diamond, declarer would ruff and the spade queen would provide the entry for the established diamond. If he opened the club suit, Venky's king would be the fulfilling trick.

It can only be a matter of conjecture what declarer should play for, if two small spades had appeared from the left in the two rounds of the suit. Surely, playing for the king on the left is the only hope for him. If that is so, he should call for the queen from the table. If it wins, he could ruff a diamond to extract West's exit card, hoping that the suit breaks 3-3, and then pray for a second 3-3 break, this time in spades, and play the third spade from hand relying on the possibility that West would be left with only clubs and would have to open up the suit. As mentioned elsewhere in this book, this would mean that both defenders held the same number of cards in each of the four suits, namely 3-3-3-4, which is very rare indeed. The odds therefore favour playing East for the ace of clubs instead.

It is also a matter of conjecture how the play would have gone if an alert West had unblocked the king on the ace of spades. Declarer will now have to guess the club position to make the contract, and should probably reason that West is more likely to find the unblock if he is looking at the ace of clubs rather than the queen. So when he continues with the nine of spades and West contributes the ten, instead of winning with the queen and playing a club to his king, declarer should prefer to duck the second spade. East will have to overtake with the jack to prevent his partner from being end-played and then declarer will play low on the forced club return.

Honestly, these are matters of conjecture as to what would happen at the table, if a different layout existed. The fact remains that something good did happen at the table, and Venky was able to make his contract. We can only say that it perhaps is a case of fulfilled hope rather than a successful specific plan of play. But, knowing Venky as I do, I am sure he would have made those plays that were available to him (if the layout were different) as mentioned in the last paragraph.

The full deal is illustrated below.

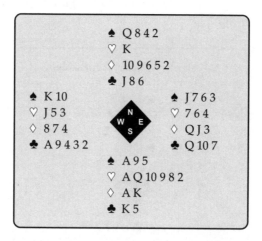

Survivors flourish on slim chances.

THE ROAD TO TEN
COULD BE DIFFICULT

Sunit Choksi is a very tall, young man. If he had taken to basketball early in life, he probably would have played for LA Lakers. Basketball's loss could well turn out to be Bridge's gain. Only five years into the world of top-class Bridge, Sunit has already played in the quarter-finals of the Bermuda Bowl and reached the Round of Sixteen in the 2002 World Championships in Montreal.

As often happens with young stars, there is just a suspicion of restlessness in this young man. If he can overcome this small weakness, it is my considered opinion that Sunit will go a long way in the world of Bridge.

Dealer East. None Vulnerable.

```
              ♠ J 5 4
              ♡ A 8 5 4
              ◇ A Q 8 2
              ♣ Q 2
                    N
                 W     E
                    S
              ♠ A K 9 8 2
              ♡ Q 3 2
              ◇ K 4
              ♣ 8 5 4
```

West	North	East	South
		Pass	1♠
Pass	2◇	Pass	2NT
Pass	4♠	All Pass	

Contract: 4♠ by South. Lead: ♣A.

Here is Sunit in action during the Indian Team Selection Trials this year (diagram on facing page).

West leads the ace of clubs, followed by the king, and then a third club which has to be ruffed on the table. With that possible heart loser staring at him, Sunit decides to play for the double finesse in the trump suit and asks for the jack of spades from dummy. West wins with the queen and exits with the ten of diamonds which Sunit wins in hand. Although his restlessness shows, Sunit pauses for a few seconds before playing the next card. Ultimately, he plays a small heart to the ace in dummy. Why he plays that way, we shall soon know.

Winning the heart ace, Sunit leads dummy's last trump to his ace and then draws the ten from the East's hand with his king, discarding a heart from the table, West having discarded a club. This is the position:

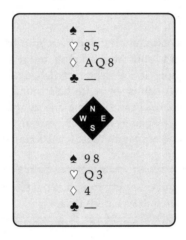

Sunit now runs his two remaining spades, discarding hearts from the table. On the nine of trumps, West lets go a small heart but on the last trump, West is clearly in trouble. After some thought, he lets go a diamond. The table's eight of diamonds is the fulfilling trick! You see, Sunit plumped for the Vienna Coup – four diamonds and the king of hearts with either defender. Most important, just recall his sequence of plays, specifically the cashing of the ace of hearts without which the Vienna Coup does not become operational!

Here is the full deal:

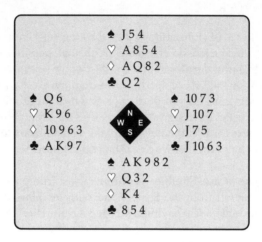

```
                    ♠ J 5 4
                    ♡ A 8 5 4
                    ◇ A Q 8 2
                    ♣ Q 2
    ♠ Q 6                         ♠ 10 7 3
    ♡ K 9 6            N          ♡ J 10 7
    ◇ 10 9 6 3      W     E       ◇ J 7 5
    ♣ A K 9 7          S          ♣ J 10 6 3
                    ♠ A K 9 8 2
                    ♡ Q 3 2
                    ◇ K 4
                    ♣ 8 5 4
```

The club lead and continuation gained a trump trick for the defence because dummy had to ruff the third club, but it also helped declarer find the winning line. If West had switched to a diamond after winning the first two clubs, or if he had found an unlikely initial diamond lead, the contract can still be made by squeezing West, but if declarer cashes the top spades, felling the queen, he will probably fall back on the losing line of playing East for the king of hearts.

> The Austrians must be very romantic people. Legend has it that the Vienna Coup was born there.

BRING HOME THE SMILES

One of my favourite Indian Bridge players is Anil Padhye. He runs a printing business in Bombay and was a member of the Indian team which finished in the top ten in the Turin Bermuda Bowl.

I first met Anil at the Bridge table some time in the late seventies and was immediately taken with his boyish smile. He was young then, but his smile has remained intact over all these years. The only thing that has changed about him is that he wears glasses these days. Remarkably likeable at and away from the table, it is a delight to sit behind him and watch him play. Quick on the uptake, his pleasantness is almost contagious when a match is in progress. Here is Anil in action:

Dealer South. E/W Vulnerable.

- ♠ Q 10 3 2
- ♡ A K Q J 2
- ◇ 10 3
- ♣ A Q

```
      N
   W     E
      S
```

- ♠ A 7 4
- ♡ 10 5 4 3
- ◇ A 9 2
- ♣ K J 3

West	North	East	South
			1NT
Pass	2♣	Pass	2♡
Pass	3♣	Pass	3♡
Pass	4♣	Pass	4◇
Pass	6♡	All Pass	

Contract: 6♡ by South. Lead: ♠9

The 1NT opener showed 12-14 points, 3♣ asked for pattern, 3♡ showed a 3-4-3-3 shape, 4♣ and 4◇ were cue bids.

Sitting South, Anil received the lead of the nine of spades; the ten was played from dummy, East put up the jack and Anil won with the ace. Making short work of the deal, Anil drew two rounds of trumps, both defenders following. He then cashed his club winners discarding dummy's losing diamond, and continued by leading a spade towards the table. When West followed small, his trade-mark smile for all to see, Anil asked of no-one in particular: "Do I have a choice?" and immediately asked for a low spade from dummy. The king came down from the right and Anil was home.

The full layout:

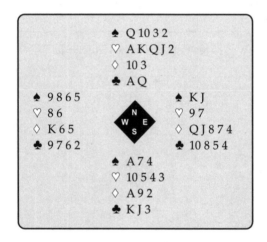

Match over, I asked Anil "Were you not helped by the lead?"

"You may not be aware, Jay, that some of these players are quite capable of leading the nine from a holding of king-nine-small, even in a slam contract."

"How would you have played the hand on, say, a diamond lead? Is there not an additional chance if hearts break 2-2?"

"Tell me."

"Win the diamond, cash one round of trumps with one of dummy's honours as a precaution, cash three clubs discarding dummy's diamond loser, ruff a diamond high, back to hand with the trump ten to confirm the 2-2 break, ruff the last diamond on the table. Now lead a spade to the ace in hand, then play a low spade towards the table and watch West's card closely. If it is the king or the jack, your problem is solved. If it is a small spade, insert the ten. You will be beaten when West ducks from K-x-x and also when East started with three or more spades including the king and the jack. In all other cases you will succeed – whether either hand holds the doubleton king or jack (if East wins the second spade and he had started with only two, it is a ruff-and-discard position), or it is West who has the jack, for example J-x-x. An early club ruff will beat you, of course, but the odds are with you, not against you. Isn't that so?"

"Yes. Jay, why don't you start playing Bridge again?"

"And make an ass of myself? I can play Bridge only if I know all fifty-two cards and the Tournament Director allows me half an hour per deal. But let me tell you something. If you promise to get two scullery-maids as our opponents, I will play with you as a partner just for old times' sake."

"What are 'scullery-maids'?"

"Read Plum's books."

"Who is Plum?"

"Pelham Grenville Wodehouse."

> The two surest ways of bringing the smiles back to our faces are (a) to read Plum's books and (b) to play Bridge.